Impact of a Uniform Formulary on Military Health System Prescribers

Baseline Survey Results

Terri Tanielian
Katherine Harris
Ana Suárez
Renée Labor
Melissa Bradley
Sidney Atkinson
Peter Glassman

Prepared for the Office of the Secretary of Defense

National Defense Research Institute | RAND Health

RAND

The research described in this report was sponsored by the Office of the Secretary of Defense (OSD). The research was conducted jointly by RAND Health's Center for Military Health Policy Research and the Forces and Resources Policy Center of the National Defense Research Institute, a federally funded research and development center supported by the OSD, the Joint Staff, the unified commands, and the defense agencies under contracts DASW01-95-C-0059 and DASW01-01-C-0004, "Pharmacy Benefits Program Redesign: Military Health System Prescriber Survey," Peter Glassman and Lee Hilborne, Principal Investigators.

Library of Congress Cataloging-in-Publication Data

Impact of a uniform formulary on military health system prescribers : baseline survey results / Terri Tanielian ... [et al.].
    p. ; cm.
    "MR-1615."
    Includes bibliographical references.
    ISBN 0-8330-3312-3 (pbk.)
    1. Pharmacy, Military—United States. 2. Medicine—Formulae, receipts, prescriptions. 3. Pharmacopoeias—United States. 4. Drugs—United States—Cost control. 5. United States—Armed Forces—Appropriations and expenditures. I. Tanielian, Terri L. II. Rand Corporation.
    [DNLM: 1. Insurance, Pharmaceutical Services. 2. Military Medicine—economics. 3. Drug Costs. 4. Formularies. 5. Pharmacy and Therapeutics Committee. 6. Physician's Practice Patterns. UH 423 I34 2003]

UH423.I47 2003
355.3'45'0973—dc21

                                      2002153674

Published 2003 by RAND
1700 Main Street, P.O. Box 2138, Santa Monica, CA 90407-2138
1200 South Hayes Street, Arlington, VA 22202-5050
201 North Craig Street, Suite 202, Pittsburgh, PA 15213-1516
RAND URL: http://www.rand.org/
To order RAND documents or to obtain additional information, contact Distribution Services: Telephone: (310) 451-7002; Fax: (310) 451-6915; Email: order@rand.org

RAND 1700 Main Street, PO Box 2138, Santa Monica, CA 90407-2138

ERRATA

PUBLICATIONS DEPARTMENT

February 23, 2004

TO: Recipients of Impact of a Uniform Formulary on Military Health System Prescribers: Baseline Survey Results, by Tanielian et al. (MR-1615-OSD)

FROM: Publications Department

Begin page 45. Replace values in Table 5.1 as follows:

Professional Category: Physician, Unweighted N = 207

Professional Category: Physician, Weighted N = 200

Practice Setting: Clinic, Unweighted N = 152

Practice Setting: Clinic, Weighted N = 164

Practice Setting: Other, Unweighted N = 29

Practice Setting: Other, Weighted N = 38

Type of Practice: Solo practice, Weighted N = 64

Type of Practice: Single-speciality group, Unweighted N = 107

Type of Practice: Single-speciality group, Weighted N = 120

Type of Practice: Multi-speciality group, Unweighted N = 30

Type of Practice: Other, Unweighted N = 12

Preface

The Military Health System (MHS) has approximately 8.7 million eligible beneficiaries. These beneficiaries include active duty military personnel and their family members, retired military personnel and their family members, and surviving family members of deceased military personnel. In 2001, the Department of Defense (DoD) spent just over $2 billion on pharmacy benefits. Much like the private health care sector, the MHS has experienced a rapid growth in pharmaceutical expenditures, which have increased an average of 17 percent a year over the past six years. Both the DoD and the U.S. Congress have identified the MHS pharmacy benefit as an area for reform.

To this end, Section 701 of the National Defense Authorization Act for Fiscal Year 2000 requires the Secretary of Defense to establish an effective, efficient, and integrated pharmacy benefits program. According to the legislation, titled the Pharmacy Benefits Redesign Program, "The pharmacy benefits program shall include a uniform formulary of pharmaceutical agents which shall assure the availability of pharmaceutical agents in the complete range of therapeutic classes. . . ." The Act further specifies that "[t]he uniform formulary will be applicable to all prescribers within the facilities of the uniformed services (i.e., military treatment facilities [MTFs]) and the TRICARE program. The pharmaceutical agents on the formulary will be available through the MTFs and retail pharmacies designated or eligible under the TRICARE program, as well as the National Mail Order Pharmacy program."

Thus, under the new pharmacy benefit program, the Secretary of Defense must submit to Congress the results of surveys of TRICARE prescribers (physicians, physician assistants, and nurse practitioners with prescribing privileges) who practice at MTFs or at TRICARE network facilities. The legislation specifically requires two confidential surveys on the uniform formulary, one conducted pre-implementation and one conducted post-implementation. RAND's National Defense Research Institute was asked by the TRICARE Management Activity to design and conduct the prescriber survey mandated by the statute.

The survey of clinicians was designed to assess how prescribers who work in MTFs or who are under the supervision of TRICARE contractors perceive formulary restrictions. The baseline survey discussed in this report attempts to gauge prescribers' perceptions of the formularies' impact on clinical decisions, aggregate cost, quality of care, and accessibility of health care provided to MHS beneficiaries. To inform future implementation and monitoring of the uniform formulary system, the study also seeks to gather information on prescribers' perceptions of the rationale behind formulary systems within the MHS.

This report was prepared at the request of the study's sponsor to document the baseline survey effort and describe the survey findings. Basic univariate and some bivariate analyses are presented to highlight differences between the survey subsamples. The report's primary intended audience is the sponsoring office. However, this research should also interest defense health policymakers and those in pharmacy benefits management in both the private and public health care sectors.

This work is sponsored by the Health Program Analysis and Evaluation Unit of the TRICARE Management Activity under the Assistant Secretary of Defense for Health Affairs. The project is being carried out jointly by RAND Health's Center for Military Health Policy Research and the Forces and Resources Policy Center of the National Defense Research Institute. The latter is a federally funded research and development center sponsored by the Office of the Secretary of Defense, the Joint Staff, the unified commands, and the defense agencies.

Comments on this report are welcome and may be addressed to Terri Tanielian at territ@rand.org. For more information on RAND's Forces and Resources Policy Center, contact the center's director, Susan Everingham, at 310-393-0411, extension 7654, or at susan_everingham@rand.org.

Contents

Appendix

Figures

Tables

Summary

Background

Over the past few decades, pharmaceuticals have become increasingly important in the delivery of medical care. They have also represented one of the fastest growing components of both U.S. civilian and Department of Defense (DoD) health care expenditures. Several factors have contributed to the acceleration of pharmacy costs, including the pace at which new drugs enter the market, the prices of these new drugs, and the increasing availability of prescription drug benefits through private insurance.

In recent years, service delivery organizations that purchase drugs on behalf of beneficiaries have begun to manage the purchase and dispensing of medications more aggressively through what is typically referred to as "pharmacy benefits management" or "formulary management." This process typically entails managing pharmaceutical care through the development of a *formulary* (i.e., a list of covered drugs) and the implementation of processes to monitor and control access to those drugs. More than 90 percent of health maintenance organizations (HMOs) use some type of formulary process to manage pharmacy benefits (Hoescht, 1999).

Formulary processes can be in the form of either "closed" or "open" systems. A *closed formulary* is a system that offers a limited set of selected pharmaceutical products, with other non-formulary drugs made available only by waiver or exemption. An *open formulary* is a system in which the availability of drugs is based on their status as generic, preferred, or non-preferred pharmaceuticals. Pharmacy benefits are also managed through the amount of co-payments, with different, or tiered, price structures for various drugs.

Determination of the actual drugs to be included on a formulary or preferred drug list is typically delegated to a Pharmacy and Therapeutics (P&T) committee—a representative group of clinicians, primarily physicians and pharmacists, for the health plan. Health plans and insurers have frequently delegated the task of pharmacy benefits or formulary development to pharmacy benefit managers (PBMs).

The MHS can move toward a more integrated formulary (i.e., a list of covered drugs) through the use of prior authorization requirements and uniform limitations on certain pharmaceuticals, such as limitations that would be monitored by the DoD's on-line national pharmacy data transaction system. These requirements and limitations would be overseen by a central pharmacy benefit management group. However, the DoD's ability to adopt a Uniform Formulary (UF) for all its MTFs has several practical constraints. Moreover, whether and how the DoD will be able to apply a Uniform Formulary to health care providers outside the traditional boundaries of the highly structured MTFs (such as TRICARE contract providers) is unclear.

There are many advantages and disadvantages to formulary systems. On the one hand, they represent an opportunity to incorporate systematic reviews of scientific evidence on clinical effectiveness and cost effectiveness into coverage decisions and management activities, thereby potentially improving health outcomes while reducing costs. On the other hand, overly restrictive formularies may potentially reduce the quality of care by limiting a patient's access to clinically indicated medicines.

The long-term effects of formularies on patient care and health outcomes are largely unknown. A number of studies[1] suggest that formulary policies can reduce health plans' pharmacy costs without impinging on patient care. However, other studies[2] have highlighted potential adverse consequences of arbitrarily restricting access to medications.

DoD Pharmacy Program Redesign

Section 701 of the National Defense Authorization Act (NDAA) for Fiscal Year (FY) 2000 (Public Law 106-65, codified at Title 10, United States Code, Section 1074g), directs the DoD to establish a single Uniform Formulary to govern Military Health System (MHS) beneficiaries' access to pharmaceuticals. The military health benefit is organized and delivered through two systems in two distinct settings—the *direct-care system* (with care delivered by TRICARE in military owned and operated treatment facilities, i.e., MTFs) and the *purchased-care system* (with care delivered by civilian providers outside MTFs under contract to TRICARE, also known as network providers). Both systems provide

[1]Foulke and Siepler, 1990; Ganz and Saksa, 1997; Dearing et al., 1998; McCombs and Nichol, 1993; Gold et al., 1989; Weiner, Lyles, and Steinwachs, 1991; Futterman, Fillit, and Roglieri, 1997; and Monane et al., 1998.

[2]Soumerai et al., 1991; Kozma, Reeder, and Lingle, 1990; Horn, 1996; Horn, Sharkey, and Phillips-Harris, 1998.

military beneficiaries with access to pharmaceuticals and currently have very different pharmacy management activities. The Uniform Formulary Program segment of the Pharmacy Benefits Redesign Program, as legislated by Congress, will require an integration of these two systems and the development of additional administrative systems.

Prior to 1999, no single entity within the DoD had responsibility for administering and coordinating pharmacy programs (U.S. General Accounting Office, 1999a). Since then, the DoD has chartered the PharmacoEconomic Center under TRICARE and created and implemented the Pharmacy Data Transaction Service, which is an electronic database designed to track prescriptions dispensed across the MTFs, network retail pharmacies, and the National Mail Order Pharmacy (NMOP).

Work is still under way to implement all requirements of the NDAA legislation and to introduce the UF across the MHS. The details of the UF are still in the rule-making and comment stage as of this writing. The proposed legislation is subject to change during the comment period and will not be considered final until it is published in the *Federal Register*.

The proposed rule introduces a three-tier co-payment structure based upon a pharmaceutical agent's classification in the UF (i.e., generic, formulary, or non-formulary) and the point of service from which the agent is acquired (i.e., an MTF, retail network pharmacy, retail non-network pharmacy, or the NMOP). For the direct-care system (i.e., drugs dispensed at the MTF), the proposed UF will resemble an expanded basic core formulary (BCF) and will continue to allow local MTF P&T committees to make additions to the formulary based on the scope of care. For the NMOP (for prescriptions written by either a direct-care provider or purchased-care provider), the proposed UF will make non-formulary medications available at the third-tier co-payment amount. In the retail network pharmacies (again, for prescriptions written by either direct-care or purchased-care providers), the UF will make 30-day supplies of non-formulary medications available at the third-tier co-payment amount.

The proposed UF program will represent a major management shift in the purchased-care system, in which formularies, currently, are open and offer few opportunities for the DoD to manage the cost of pharmacy benefits. Thus, through the proposed UF, the DoD will gain the ability to determine how prescriptions are dispensed, from a cost standpoint, in the purchased-care sector. The DoD will gain this ability through higher co-payments, which will create incentives for beneficiaries to opt for preferred formulary medications and to consider filling their prescriptions for such medications through the MTF pharmacies or through the NMOP.

Survey of Military Health System Prescribers

To assess the impact of the uniform formulary on the care delivered in the Military Health System, particularly in regard to perceived access to pharmaceuticals, Congress required two surveys of MHS prescribers, one prior to UF implementation (the baseline survey) and another following the UF implementation (the follow-up survey). At the request of the TRICARE Management Activity (TMA) and in compliance with Section 701 of the NDAA for FY 2000, RAND conducted the first of these surveys in mid-2001. The purpose of the first survey effort was to measure and evaluate the perceptions of prescribers who practice at MTFs and prescribers who practice under TRICARE contract in the civilian sector. The survey sought feedback regarding obstacles prescribers face in providing beneficiaries with formulary medications, non-formulary medications (or "non-preferred" medications as they may currently be called), and quality pharmacotherapeutic care. The baseline survey described in this report assesses how prescribers' perceptions of and attitudes toward formularies may be currently influencing their decisions on prescribing pharmaceutical products.

Because military benefits (including pharmacy benefits) are delivered in two distinct systems—direct-care and purchased-care—and because these two systems currently have two different formulary management systems, two separate survey instruments were designed for MHS prescribers.[3] One survey instrument was aimed at TRICARE prescribers working within the direct-care system in MTFs, and a second survey instrument was aimed at prescribers who provide services to military beneficiaries at network facilities under contract to TRICARE.

Seven hundred MTF (i.e., direct-care) prescribers and 600 network (i.e., purchased-care) prescribers were sampled using data obtained from claims records for fall 2000. We drew a stratified sample within each of the two target populations to ensure representation of specific analytic groups of interest (e.g., non-M.D. providers, specialists, and others). Prescribers were asked a series of questions about their knowledge of and degree of familiarity with formularies, formulary development, and management practices. They were also asked

---

[3]"Prescribers" as defined by the FY 2000 NDAA are physicians, physician assistants, and nurse practitioners with prescribing privileges.

specific questions about their perceptions of the impact of formulary management on their own prescribing behavior and the quality of care provided to their patients. Participants were also questioned about their background and medical practice. Sixty-nine percent of eligible MTF (direct-care) prescribers and 39 percent of eligible network (purchased care) prescribers responded.

Conclusions

MTF prescribers who responded to the survey reported a high degree of familiarity with the formulary and formulary management practices in place at their own MTFs. In general, MTF respondents perceived formulary management as contributing toward quality of care and agreed that controlling costs through such formulary management is important.

Network prescribers who responded to the survey reported interacting with multiple formularies and formulary management practices. Network respondents reported less familiarity and comfort with formulary lists and the rules governing their use. They did not believe that formulary management was contributing to the quality of care they provided.

Some differences were observed within each sample. For example, within the direct-care system, primary-care providers reported having a higher level of familiarity and greater comfort with formulary management techniques than did secondary-care providers. Direct-care providers within smaller MTFs also reported greater familiarity with the activities of P&T committees and with the rules governing non-formulary prescriptions at their MTF than did direct-care providers at larger MTFs. Within the purchased-care system, primary-care providers interacted with a greater number of preferred or formulary drug lists than did their secondary-care provider counterparts.

A follow-up RAND survey, which will be administered approximately six months subsequent to implementation of the UF, will assess changes in prescribing behaviors and in prescribers' perceptions and attitudes about formulary management in general, as well as assess prescribers' actual experiences with the DoD Uniform Formulary specifically.

Acknowledgments

The authors wish to thank several individuals for their guidance and support in carrying out this work. We are especially grateful to Colonel William Davies, director of the DoD Pharmacy Benefit Program, for providing valuable information with regard to the DoD pharmacy programs, feedback on survey instruments, and insight into the results. We also acknowledge the guidance of Lee Hilborne, M.D., who served as a mentor and co-principal investigator for the survey. We thank Ross Anthony for his leadership and advice in making this effort successful. We also acknowledge the support of the project officer, Lieutenant Colonel Thomas Williams, and the staff within TMA's Health Program Analysis and Evaluation office. We would also like to thank John Downs, M.D., and Jesse Malkin, M.Phil., Ph.D., for their review and valuable comments, and Nancy DelFavero for her editing work on this report.

Finally, we also thank the prescribers within the MHS who took the time to complete the survey instrument; without their responses, this report would not have been possible.

Acronyms and Abbreviations

BCF	Basic Core Formulary
BRAC	Base realignment and closure
CHCS	Composite Health Care System
DoD	Department of Defense
DSC–P	Defense Supply Center–Philadelphia
DTC	Direct-to-consumer (marketing)
FDA	Food and Drug Administration
FY	Fiscal year
GAO	U.S. Government Accounting Office
HCPR	Health Care Provider Record
HCSR	Health Care Service Record
HMO	Health maintenance organization
HPAE	Health program analysis and evaluation
ID	Identification
MHS	Military Health System
MTF	Military treatment facility
N	Number (in sample)
N/A	Not applicable
NDAA	National Defense Authorization Act
NMOP	National Mail Order Pharmacy
OMB	Office of Management and Budget
OTC	Over-the-counter (medications)

p	Probability (of difference being due to chance)
PA/APN	Physician assistant/Advanced practice nurse
PBM	Pharmacy benefits manager
PDTS	Pharmacy Data Transaction Service
PEC	PharmacoEconomic Center
P&T	Pharmacy and Therapeutics (committee)
SADR	Standard Ambulatory Data Record
SD	Standard deviation
TMA	TRICARE Management Activity
TRICARE	The Department of Defense managed care program
UF	Uniform Formulary
VA	Department of Veterans Affairs

1. Introduction

The National Defense Authorization Act (NDAA) for Fiscal Year (FY) 2000,[1] titled the Pharmacy Benefits Redesign Program, requires the Department of Defense (DoD) to integrate its pharmacy programs by creating a single Uniform Formulary (UF) to govern Military Health System (MHS) beneficiaries' access to outpatient pharmaceuticals. The proposed UF (i.e., a uniform list of covered drugs) introduces a three-tier co-payment price structure based on the classification of a drug as generic, formulary, or non-formulary and based on the point of service (i.e., military treatment facility [MTF], retail network pharmacy, retail non-network pharmacy, or the National Mail Order Pharmacy [NMOP]).

Although the schedule for implementation of the UF itself has not been finalized, the NDAA mandates that certain requirements be met when the proposed UF is implemented. Those requirements include the establishment of the following:

- Procedures for evaluating the relative clinical effectiveness and cost effectiveness of alternative pharmaceutical agents[2] and for incorporating the assessments of alternative pharmaceuticals into decisions on the content of the formulary

- Procedures to assure patient access to clinically appropriate non-formulary pharmaceutical agents

- Procedures for prior authorization to prescribe a drug not included in the UF, when required

- Cost-sharing determinations (that is, the share the patient or sponsor will be required to pay) for all classes of drugs (i.e., generic, formulary, and non-formulary agents)

- A Pharmacy and Therapeutics (P&T) committee charged with developing and maintaining a list of pharmaceutical agents covered by MHS health programs

---

[1] Public Law 106-65, codified at Title 10, U.S. Code, Section 1074g.

[2] "Alternative pharmaceutical agents" in this context refers to agents other than the most costly or newest agents or those most likely to be prescribed. These agents may include generic brands, lower-cost or older analogs, or, in some cases, agents with another mode of action.

2

- A Uniform Formulary Beneficiary Advisory Panel charged with overseeing formulary development and with overseeing the implementation of and subsequent changes to the UF

- A Pharmacy Data Transaction Service (PDTS)—a database that will track all MTF, NMOP, and network prescriptions

- A prescriber survey, with "prescribers" defined as physicians, physician assistants, and nurse practitioners with prescribing privileges who are subject to the UF.

The TRICARE Management Activity (TMA) asked RAND's National Defense Research Institute to design and conduct the prescriber surveys required by the NDAA statute. The NDAA legislation specifically requires two confidential surveys, one conducted pre-implementation and another conducted post-implementation. Data from the initial baseline (pre-implementation) survey are summarized in this report. The follow-up (post-implementation) survey will be administered approximately six months subsequent to implementation of the UF, which at the time of this writing was projected to occur in mid-2003.

The goal of the baseline and follow-up surveys is to measure and evaluate the perceptions of prescribers who practice at MTFs and under TRICARE contract regarding obstacles to providing beneficiaries with formulary medications, non-formulary medications (or "non-preferred" medications as they may currently be called), and quality pharmacotherapeutic care. The baseline survey, described in this report, assesses how prescribers' perceptions of and attitudes toward formularies may be currently influencing their decisions on prescribing pharmaceutical products. The follow-up survey will assess changes in prescribing behaviors and in prescribers' perceptions and attitudes about formulary management in general, as well as assess prescribers' actual experiences with the DoD UF in particular.

Specifically, these surveys are designed to answer key questions on three issues posed by the NDAA:

- **Access to clinically indicated drug therapy:** How often during the most recent fiscal year did prescribers attempt to prescribe non-formulary or non-preferred prescription drugs, how often were they able to do so, and were covered beneficiaries able to get such prescriptions filled without undue delay?

- **Formulary development:** To what extent do prescribers understand formulary processes and the reasons why the MTFs or the civilian contractors (providers) outside MTFs prefer certain pharmaceuticals to others?

- **Formulary decisions and patient care:** What has been the impact of formulary restrictions on clinical decisions? What are prescribers' opinions of a formulary's impact on the aggregate cost, quality, and accessibility of health care provided to covered beneficiaries?

The primary purpose of this report is to describe RAND's progress on the survey effort to date. In Chapter 2, we describe the proposed UF in more detail. We provide background information on the formulary systems in place prior to the FY 2000 NDAA, which provides the context for measuring the impact of the UF. In Chapter 3, we discuss development of the survey instrument and our sampling strategy. In Chapter 4, we provide an overview of our fielding and implementation methods and response analysis. In Chapter 5, we present the survey responses for each sample population, (i.e., direct-care prescribers and purchased-care prescribers), and in Chapter 6, we summarize our findings and conclusions and discuss the next steps in this research.

2. Study Background

Increasing Use and Cost of Pharmaceuticals

Over the past few decades, pharmaceuticals have taken on an increasingly important role in the delivery of medical care. Pharmaceuticals are also one of the fastest growing components of U.S. health care expenditures (Teitelbaum et al., 1999). Between 1990 and 1997, drug expenditures grew at an average annual rate of 9 percent while total health care expenditures grew at a rate of 5 percent (Hogan, Ginsburg, and Gabel, 2000). By 1998, drug expenditures were growing at an annual rate of 14.3 percent; by comparison, total health care expenditures were growing at an annual rate of 4.5 percent (Hogan, Ginsburg, and Gabel, 2000). More recently, drug expenditures have been surpassed by hospital costs as the fastest growing component of health care expenditures; nevertheless, drug expenditures remain a significant portion of overall U.S. health care costs (Strunk, Ginsburg, and Gabel, 2001).

According to data from IMS Health (a leading provider of pharmaceutical information; see www.imshealth.com), private-sector drug spending has increased an average of 16.1 percent per year in the past ten years and in 2000 accounted for roughly 9.4 percent of U.S. health care expenditures (Masia, 2002). The increase has been due in part to drug prices having gone up and in part to an increasing number of prescriptions being written and dispensed each year.

While drug prices have risen an average of 4 percent between 1990 and 2001 (Masia, 2002), two other factors, which we discuss next, are the most important contributors to the acceleration in pharmacy costs.

Increased Use of New Drugs

The first factor in accelerated pharmacy costs is the increasing pace at which new drugs arrive on the market. New drugs account for a disproportionate share of the growth in pharmaceutical use and expenditures. More specifically, new drugs, meaning those introduced after 1995, accounted for roughly half of the expenditure growth between 1994 and 1998 (Teitelbaum, 1999).

New drugs tend to be more expensive because they are sold under patent protection, meaning that lower-cost generic drugs cannot be prescribed as substitutes. However, in some cases, new drugs can be cost saving because they can offset their higher unit cost by reducing the need for more intensive and costly treatments, such as inpatient surgery.

Newer pharmaceuticals may also increase overall pharmacy expenditures when they are developed for previously untreatable conditions or for conditions for which older drug therapies are not well tolerated. For example, over the past decade, this issue has been especially relevant in the use of newer drugs to manage HIV/AIDS, hepatitis C, and transplant rejection. Likewise, new drugs are prescribed to treat conditions, such as wrinkled skin, obesity, or habitual smoking, previously considered to be the side effects of aging or the results of lifestyle choices.

Increased Prescription Drug Benefits and Direct-to-Consumer Marketing

The second factor contributing to the growth of pharmaceutical costs is the increasing availability of prescription drug benefits packages in health insurance policies. Over the past two decades, the proportion of drug expenditures covered by insurers has grown (U.S. Department of Health and Human Services, 2000). This growth has tended to shift drug purchase costs from consumers to insurers and likely has decreased incentives for cost-effective prescribing (Teitelbaum et al., 1999; Newhouse, 1994).

At the same time, evidence suggests that direct-to-consumer (DTC) marketing has shifted demand to some more-expensive drugs (Bozzette et al., 2001; Mintzes et al., 2002), as is believed to be the case with the allergy medication Claritin (generic name Loratadine). Consumers may not feel the impact of that shift and thus may have no incentive to request cheaper drugs if co-payments do not reflect relative differences in prices paid by their health plans. In addition, studies have demonstrated that DTC marketing, which has greatly increased since the Food and Drug Administration (FDA) issued guidelines on the subject in 1997, has greatly impacted patients' requests for pharmaceuticals and in turn has driven prescribing decisions (Mintzes et al., 2002).

It is important to note, however, that while spending for DTC marketing has increased, it represents only about 15 percent of the money spent on drug promotion and is highly concentrated on subgroups of products (Rosenthal et al.,

2002). Drug detailing[1] and other physician-oriented promotions continue to constitute the majority of marketing efforts within the pharmaceutical industry and can have a powerful impact on prescribing decisions.

Management of Pharmaceutical Benefits

Service delivery organizations that purchase drugs on behalf of beneficiaries have reacted to increasing pharmacy costs by managing the purchase and dispensing of drugs more aggressively. These activities typically take place in the context of "formulary management" or, as it is becoming more commonly known, "pharmacy benefits management." Regardless of the term, the process of managing pharmaceutical care usually includes developing a list of covered drugs or preferred drugs (that is, a *formulary* or a *preferred list,* respectively) and implementing the processes required to monitor and control access to those drugs.

In many cases, guidelines on dispensing activities (i.e., filling prescriptions) as well as rules for physicians in prescribing drugs are included in those processes. A survey of health maintenance organizations (HMOs) noted that more than 90 percent of HMOs now use some type of formulary process to manage pharmaceutical prescribing and dispensing (Hoescht, 1999).

Nearly half of all HMOs use *closed formularies* (a limited set of selected pharmaceutical products) with other non-formulary drugs made available by waiver or by exemption. Other organizations use a more-open formulary system in which the availability of drugs is based on their status as generic, preferred, or non-preferred. In these instances, the pharmacy benefits package is often managed by a co-payment system with different, or tiered, price structures for various agents. Although the terms "closed formulary" and "open formulary" are traditionally used to describe how drugs are covered, the terms are becoming less meaningful because many of the techniques for managing pharmaceuticals are similar under both circumstances (Schulman, 1996; Flagstad, 1996).

When access to some drugs is limited, responsibility for coverage decisions and oversight activities (such as ensuring appropriate prescribing and implementing pre-authorizations rules) is ultimately that of the health plan or the insurer. However, determination of the actual drugs included in a formulary or preferred list is typically delegated to a representative group of clinicians—mostly

---

[1]"Drug detailing" refers to the practice of pharmaceutical company representatives (who generally represent one or two specific medications) marketing their companies' products by visiting physicians' offices and providing free drug samples and informational materials.

physicians and pharmacists—who are typically convened by the benefit plan and are known collectively as the P&T committee. Over the past decade, health plans and insurers have frequently turned over the task of managing pharmacy benefits or formulary development to pharmacy benefits managers (PBMs). PBM activities may include any or all of the following.

Therapeutic Switching or Substitution

Therapeutic switching or *therapeutic substitution* refers to switching from one drug to another, usually on the basis of reducing costs while maintaining quality of care and, in some instances, improving clinical or therapeutic effect. Switching is often done because of price negotiations (discussed later) that secure discounts or rebates on certain drugs for health plans/insurers.

Typically, switching involves substituting a branded product with a generic version or switching one branded drug with another branded drug within the same drug class. In some cases, a therapeutic switch may be between drugs from different pharmaceutical classes or may be proposed for reasons apart from cost savings, such as safety (e.g., one drug is thought to be safer than another drug for a covered population) or convenience (one drug formulation is easier to use than another). Pharmacy programs (as part of a health plan) that utilize the switching/substitution strategy usually require permission from the patient and/or physician to switch a prescription to another drug, although specific requirements are usually determined by the P&T committee or PBM.

Step-Therapy

Step-therapy refers to programs that ensure that trials of certain drugs in a therapeutic class are prescribed before other less-cost-effective, or more-toxic, drugs are used. Step therapy also can help assure that drugs that have greater scientific evidence of efficacy are used before drugs that have less of a demonstrated benefit.

Disease Management

Disease management includes programs that focus on optimizing pharmacologic therapy (e.g., adjusting the dosage or duration of prescribed medications or improving patient adherence to dosage instructions) and non-pharmacologic therapy (e.g., providing education on beneficial lifestyle changes and self-monitoring of diseases or physical conditions). Many disease management programs concentrate on patients with chronic conditions such as diabetes mellitus or coronary disease.

Price Negotiation

In cases in which the beneficiary population is large, pharmacy managers negotiate lower drug prices with manufacturers. This process, in turn, allows pharmacy managers to offer lower prices for particular agents within a therapeutic class. The intent is to steer prescribers to lower-cost drugs by excluding higher-cost alternatives from the formulary or by charging a lower co-payment for the preferred drug relative to the costlier alternative.

Other strategies to increase the use of preferred drugs include therapeutic switching programs and sharing of cost risks between providers and health plans. Third-party PBMs typically pass cost savings on to clients and retain a portion of the rebate to cover administrative costs and to generate a profit.

Advantages and Disadvantages of Formulary Systems

On the one hand, formularies and preferred lists present an opportunity to incorporate systematic reviews of scientific evidence on clinical effectiveness and cost effectiveness into coverage decisions and management activities. The adoption and implementation of formularies or preferred lists have the potential to improve health outcomes by promoting evidence-based medicine and to reduce costs by emphasizing cost-effective drug management and volume purchasing.

On the other hand, overly restrictive formularies may potentially reduce quality of care by limiting access to clinically indicated medicines, thus increasing morbidity and/or mortality and, perhaps, causing the utilization of other types of health care. Yet, the threshold separating appropriately managed pharmaceutical benefits and overly restrictive drug availability remains unclear. Table 2.1 summarizes the potential advantages and disadvantages of formulary systems.

Before determining the extent to which a formulary should control pharmaceutical care, sufficient data are needed to inform formulary decisions and policies. Bozzette et al. (2001) found that because of a lack of critical data, few health care organizations based their coverage decisions on rigorous and systematic assessments of the comparative effectiveness and costs of various drugs, despite a strong desire to do so. Interviews that other researchers have

Table 2.1

Potential Advantages and Disadvantages of Formularies and Formulary Management Practices

Advantages	Disadvantages
Provide forum for provider education	Could increase administrative costs for the benefit plan or for the consumer and could inconvenience the beneficiary/patient or the pharmacies
Increase patient safety by reducing adverse events and interactions	
Improve quality and control costs through a systematic review of clinical and economic literature, which helps to inform coverage decisions	Reduce quality of health care and increase costs of care through restricted access
	Cause disruptions in care
Control costs by channeling market share to obtain volume discounts	

SOURCE: Blumenthal and Herdman (2000).

had with medical directors revealed a shared perception that adequate data were either lacking, not specific enough to their own organizations or covered populations, or biased because the evidence was generated by pharmaceutical manufacturers (Luce, 1995; Bozzette et al., 2001).

Research on the Impact of Formulary Systems

The long-term effects of formularies on patient care and health outcomes are largely unknown. However, a variety of studies suggests that formulary policies can benefit health plans without impinging on patient care. For example, one goal of formulary policy is to improve cost-effective prescribing either by lowering costs while maintaining quality or by improving quality while maintaining costs.

One method for testing the effects of formularies is to follow patients who have undergone a therapeutic substitution, such as the substitution of a generic formulation in place of a branded product, or who have been prescribed one branded drug in place of another. Foulke and Siepler (1990) demonstrated that switching from the anti-ulcer drug ranitidine to the anti-ulcer drug cimetidine resulted in dramatic cost savings while maintaining clinical outcomes. Ganz and Saksa (1997) found that switching between two versions of the long-acting antihypertensive agent nifedipine reduced costs and had similar outcomes before and after the switch. Dearing et al. (1998) noted a similar effect with a therapeutic switch from nifedipine to felodipine. Patel et al. (1999) found no significant differences in the percentage of patients meeting cholesterol targets before and after a change from the agent pravastatin to the similar agent lovastatin. In addition, they found no differences in quality-of-life measures, patient satisfaction, or medication tolerance.

Apart from studies on therapeutic switching, other research has shown several potential benefits of formulary policies. Those benefits include improving access to expensive drugs and reducing inappropriate use. For example, McCombs and Nichol (1993) found that outpatient drug treatment protocols that limited use of an expensive agent improved access to that medication for high-risk patients while reducing post-treatment health care expenditures. Rahal et al. (1998) found that restrictions on antibiotic choice minimized antibacterial resistance patterns. Smalley et al. (1995) found that prior authorization for selected non-steroidal anti-inflammatory drugs reduced costs but not access to appropriate care.

In addition, formulary-related activities may promote more rational drug use policies (Gold et al., 1989; Weiner, Lyles, and Steinwachs, 1991) and may increase patient safety, especially in older and more-vulnerable patients, by reducing the use of agents that have greater side effects (Futterman, Fillit, and Roglieri, 1997; Monane et al., 1998).

Despite the availability of findings from smaller-scaled focused studies, few large-scale studies on formulary-related activities have attempted to measure the impact of formularies on service use, costs, and health outcomes. The few that have done so suffer from methodological flaws. For example, in a longitudinal study of South Carolina Medicaid patients, Kozma, Reeder, and Lingle (1990) noted a negative association between expanded drug coverage and hospital admissions, resulting in a shift toward outpatient care. However, the national trend away from inpatient care and toward ambulatory care during Kozma and colleagues' study period of the mid-1980s may have confounded the study outcome. Similarly, evidence derived from the Managed Care Outcomes Project suggested an association between restrictive formularies and increased health care costs (Horn et al., 1996; Horn, Sharkey, and Phillips-Harris, 1998). However, Horn and colleagues used data from only six HMOs and were unable to control for the effects of pre-existing differences in patient populations, organizational structures, and health care utilization. Other researchers' attempts to adjust for confounding variables using statistical modeling were successful in explaining only a small part of the observed variance (Ross-Degnan and Soumerai, 1996; Kravitz and Romano, 1996).

The potential adverse consequences of arbitrarily restricting access to medications were highlighted in an influential study by Soumerai et al. (1991). They found that a stringent three-drug limit per patient had negative effects on rates of nursing home admissions of older Medicaid patients. Soumerai et al.

compared the effects of a three-drug reimbursement policy, then in effect in New Hampshire, on Medicaid patients in that state with the outcomes for a matched cohort in New Jersey that did not have a similar policy. They found that the risk of admission to a nursing home increased about twofold, although no effect on hospital admissions was seen. After the three-drug limit was rescinded, the higher rates of nursing home admissions fell back to the initially observed rates, which suggested strongly that arbitrarily capping payments on drugs shifted health expenditures to more expensive venues. In contrast, Walser, Ross-Degnan, and Soumerai (1996) concluded that the loosening of very restrictive Medicaid formularies, as a consequence of the Omnibus Reconciliation Act of 1990, led to an increased number of drugs being made available to patients, but those drugs yielded only nominal potential therapeutic benefit.

Motheral and Henderson (2000) demonstrated that a closed formulary reduced the use of brand medications within an employer plan and resulted in substantial savings to the payor; however, they noted that the time-frame limitation of the study likely resulted in a failure to detect any long-term changes in utilization and costs. While the results of this study are not generalizable to other closed formularies in other plans, the authors posit several reasons why the closed formulary reduced the use of brand medications including discretionary (i.e., unnecessary or marginal) pharmaceuticals. However, Motheral and Henderson also observed a lower rate of compliance among those in the closed formulary group who were initially taking non-formulary medications. Thus, the closed formulary may have promoted higher discontinuation rates for essential medications among formulary subjects, which could lead to adverse health effects and future cost consequences.

Taken as a whole, the three large-scale studies we just cited suggest that arbitrary decisionmaking on drug coverage and/or overly restrictive reimbursement policies may have an adverse impact on patient care. However, the studies do little to help in rendering an overall assessment of formularies in general and even less to explore how a specific organization's formulary or pharmacy benefits policy may impact patient care. This oversight is not entirely unexpected because, by their very nature, formularies are dynamic. Disentangling a formulary effect from the overall package of managed-care administrative activities that may affect physician decisions is difficult (Kreling and Mucha, 1992; Schulman et al., 1996). A number of methodological obstacles remain to be overcome when objectively evaluating the health outcomes of drug formularies and preferred lists (Rucker and Schiff, 1990).

Nonetheless, three recent studies, one by Glassman et al. (2001), one by the U.S. General Accounting Office (GAO) (2001), and one by the Institute of Medicine

(Blumenthal and Herdman, 2000), which evaluated pharmaceutical management within the Department of Veterans Affairs (VA) may have some potential relevance to the DoD. Two of these studies queried VA physicians in order to measure the perceived impact of the VA National Formulary on a range of access and patient care issues. The first study (Glassman et al., 2001) found that the majority of responding physicians did not perceive that the National Formulary adversely impacted access to pharmaceuticals, quality of care, resident training, and clinical workload. Preliminary results from the second study (U.S. General Accounting Office, 2001) were generally consistent with those of the first study, suggesting that a majority of VA physicians agree that the VA formulary contains drugs needed for patient care and that they are able to obtain approvals for necessary non-formulary drugs. Although the two studies had a somewhat different focus, both assessed physicians' attitudes about a national formulary and neither study found the relatively closed VA National Formulary to be overly restrictive. While the DoD is not proposing a closed formulary, nor is it proposing a closed system such as the VA's, the data regarding physicians' attitudes and experiences with formularies may provide some insight into how a new UF might be perceived among MHS prescribers.

Given the lack of more-objective data about the global effect of formularies, Glassman et al. (2001) have pointed out that assessing prescriber perceptions of formulary policies, by means of survey research, may assist in better understanding the impact of formulary management activities on prescribing patterns. As yet, little is known about individual prescribers' perceptions of and attitudes toward formularies and formulary management practices and the impact of those attitudes on clinical practice. As such, the baseline survey described in this report and required by Congress will provide some additional information in this regard. Until recently, survey data focused on only minor aspects of formulary care, such as providers' perceptions regarding availability of specific drugs (Hasty, Schrager, and Wrenn, 1999), or addressed only general attitudes toward cost containment (Donelan et al., 1997; Schectman et al., 1995).

The Department of Defense Pharmacy Programs

The MHS serves roughly 8.7 million beneficiaries, who include active duty military personnel and their family members, retired military personnel and their family members, and surviving family members of deceased military personnel. The MHS is dedicated to pursuing two related goals: (1) ensuring military readiness through overseeing the health and well-being of active duty military personnel and (2) assuring that active duty dependents and retired military families have access to health care services. The NDAA of FY 2001 expanded TRICARE benefits to also include Medicare-eligible military retirees.

The military health benefit is organized and delivered through two systems in two distinct settings. In the *direct-care system*, the military provides direct care to active duty personnel and military beneficiaries in military-owned and operated treatment facilities (i.e., in MTFs). In the *purchased-care system*, the military health benefit pays for authorized care rendered by civilian providers outside MTFs. Both systems are administered through the TRICARE program. Part of the TRICARE program includes providing access to pharmaceuticals.

The DoD processes approximately 65 million prescriptions annually. In recent years, DoD expenditures on pharmaceuticals have risen dramatically, mirroring trends in the civilian sector. For example, in 2001, the DoD spent just over $2 billion on pharmaceuticals, which represents a 28 percent increase from 2000. In April 2001, the DoD introduced a new pharmacy benefit for Medicare-eligible military retirees, greatly expanding the availability of drugs to this population and increasing the DoD's exposure to such costs. Costs have risen steadily over the past several years, from a 7 percent increase in 1996 to a 28 percent increase in 2001 (a 17 percent average increase over the six-year period).

MHS beneficiaries may obtain prescriptions at one of the following four points of service: (1) outpatient pharmacies at MTFs; (2) the NMOP, administered by a single private contractor; (3) retail network pharmacies established by TRICARE contractors; and (4) non-network retail pharmacies. Each program has its own purchasing and distribution system, patient cost-sharing requirements, and process for establishing formulary inclusion and access to non-formulary drugs.

Currently, 587 MTF pharmacies serve the three military services and 15 TRICARE health service regions. MTF pharmacies process approximately 52 million prescriptions annually (representing roughly 80 percent of all prescriptions processed for MTF beneficiaries).[2] In 2001, drug expenditures in MTF pharmacies totaled approximately $1.2 billion. In addition, 40,000 retail pharmacies serve four separate managed-care-support contract networks under TRICARE. These pharmacies process approximately 12 million prescriptions annually. In 2001, drug expenditures in retail pharmacies totaled approximately $500 million. The NMOP processes approximately 1.5 million prescriptions annually. NMOP drug expenditures were approximately $300 million in 2001.

---

[2]Information about DoD expenditures for pharmaceuticals was drawn from presentations given by Colonel William Davies to medical residents at Baylor University, May 9, 2001, and by Colonel Daniel Remund, director of the DoD Pharmacoeconomic Center, during a TRICARE conference in February 2002 in Washington, D.C.

Prior to 1999, no single entity within the DoD had responsibility for administering and coordinating pharmacy programs (U.S. General Accounting Office, 1999a). The DoD took an important step in this direction by chartering under TRICARE the PharmacoEconomic Center (PEC), whose stated mission is "to improve the clinical, economic, and humanistic outcomes of drug therapy in support of the readiness and managed care missions of the MHS." The PEC is engaged in a range of activities that relate to this mission. These activities include conducting pharmacoeconomic studies, providing analytic support to the DoD and NMOP P&T committees, providing customer support to users of the PDTS, assisting in the development and management of pharmacy-related information systems, and publishing an educational newsletter targeted to prescribers and other stakeholders that covers cost-effective drug therapies. Other PEC activities include assisting the Defense Supply Center–Philadelphia (DSC-P), a defense agency that negotiates prices with individual pharmaceutical manufacturers, and VA Pharmacy Benefits Management in contract negotiations with pharmaceutical manufacturers and participating in the development of pharmaceutical-related components of clinical practice guidelines.[3]

The following subsections briefly describe the DoD's three prescription systems—the direct-care system, the purchased-care system, and the NMOP.

The Direct-Care System

Prescribing of pharmaceuticals in the MTF system is governed by a national, yet locally tailored, formulary system.

First, a DoD P&T committee establishes a "core" formulary that is shared by all MTFs. The Basic Core Formulary (BCF)[4] established in April 1998 contains the minimum set of drugs that each MTF pharmacy must have on its formulary to support the primary-care scope of practice for primary-care manager enrollment sites (TRICARE Prime provider sites). The BCF contains two closed therapeutic classes—HMG CoA (3-hydroxy-3 methylglutaryl co-enzyme A) reductase inhibitors (otherwise known as "statins") and nonsedating antihistamines. Adhering to these closed classes, under the DoD's National Pharmaceutical Contracts, provides system-wide cost avoidance.

To supplement the core formulary, local MTF P&T committees can add drugs to create site-specific MTF formularies that are tailored to the particular mission of

---

[3]The PEC Web site describes this program more fully (www.pec.ha.osd.mil/PEC_Chrt.htm).
[4]Information on the Basic Core Formulary was found at www.pec.ha.osd.mil/ac01001.htm (last accessed July 2, 2002).

and scope of practice within that MTF. However, the DoD mandates generic substitution when available.

MTFs obtain drugs through the DSC-P. In general, the DoD obtains highly competitive prices relative to those granted to health plans and pharmaceutical benefits manufacturers that are as much as 70 percent less than the average wholesale prices (U.S. General Accounting Office, 1999a).[5]

Despite relatively low unit prices for pharmaceuticals, defense budget cuts during the 1990s and an increasing demand for prescription drugs put pressure on MTF drug budgets. The need to control pharmacy costs, combined with DoD rules assuring that all beneficiary groups have equal access to drugs, has resulted in MTFs dropping formulary coverage of selected popular and expensive drugs and not adding newer drugs as they have gained FDA approval (U.S. General Accounting Office, 1999a).

Drugs that are not on MTF formularies can be made available through a non-formulary waiver. Prescribers can obtain non-formulary drugs for their patients by either one of two methods. The first method is called a "special drug request" (sometimes also referred to as a "special patient purchase"). Procedures for obtaining drugs through this method vary and are left to the local DoD base commander's discretion. A frequent practice is for the prescriber to complete a special drug request form and forward it through departmental clinical directors to the MTF pharmacy. The chief pharmacist is usually delegated the authority to make interim approval (thus immediate purchase) or interim denial decisions, pending the next P&T committee meeting. The P&T committee then recommends approval or denial; appeals of denials are made to the MTF's Hospital Executive Committee and the commander. An alternative method requires the patient to fill the prescription though a retail pharmacy, which bypasses clinical directors, the P&T committee, Hospital Executive Committee, and commander. This practice, in addition to bypassing all institutional oversight, is very costly to the DoD because drugs dispensed in this way do not receive the substantial discounts available to the government under federal pricing.

Prescriptions written by non-MTF prescribers (whether affiliated with TRICARE or not) for medications not covered by the MTF formulary cannot be filled at MTF pharmacies. In simple cases, the pharmacist can call the prescribing doctor and have the prescription changed to one that is on the MTF formulary. At present, all beneficiaries have the option to get their prescriptions filled through a

---

[5]Average wholesale prices often significantly overstate prevailing prices in the marketplace after rebates are taken into account. As such, 70 percent below average wholesale price may not be below the market average price for some drugs after rebates.

network retail pharmacy for a nominal co-payment. However, prior to FY 2001, Medicare-eligible military retirees not eligible for base realignment and closure (BRAC) benefits did not have this option.[6] Thus, rewriting prescriptions that needed to be filled in MTFs created additional demands for the already limited appointment times. Prescribers are discouraged from submitting special patient purchase requests on behalf of patients who are being treated outside the MTF. These requests place MTF doctors in a precarious position from a quality of care perspective.[7] Little is currently known about any formal or ad hoc processes to deal with these requests and the additional workload they entail.

The Purchased-Care System

The fees that the DoD pays to TRICARE managed-care support contractors cover the cost of prescription drugs dispensed in retail network and non-network pharmacies. Providers who treat TRICARE beneficiaries outside MTFs basically have an open formulary with which they can prescribe all FDA-approved drugs, with the exception of drugs intended to treat conditions explicitly excluded from coverage under TRICARE benefits, such as those for smoking cessation and weight loss. Some TRICARE contractors have asserted that increased restrictions on MTF formularies are to blame for overruns in pharmaceutical budgets because prescriptions for items not available in MTFs are filled at retail pharmacies, where the cost savings to the DoD are not as large (U.S. General Accounting Office, 1999a).

While the TRICARE formulary is currently unrestricted for network providers, the prescribing practices of almost all community providers, including those who treat TRICARE beneficiaries, are increasingly governed by formularies and pharmacy benefits policies. In many cases, community providers are confronted with a multitude of formularies and preferred lists because most of those providers care for patient populations covered by a variety of insurers. Because no standard formulary exists across health plans, prescribers are exposed to numerous policies and prescribing regulations. Anecdotal evidence suggests that community providers are increasingly frustrated with the limits that formularies place on their prescribing practices and perceive those limits to be arbitrary rather than based on sound clinical and cost-effectiveness criteria.

---

[6]Prior to FY 2001, Medicare-eligible retirees living in catchment areas for closed MTFs were eligible to use the NMOP as part of the BRAC agreements.

[7]Colonel William Davies, director, DoD Pharmacy Programs, personal communications, September 8, 2000.

18

Several recent studies support these perceptions and suggest that formulary inclusion decisions are driven in large part by volume discounts obtained when plans steer market share toward a particular drug in a therapeutic class (Schulman et al., 1996; Bozzette et al., 2001). These changes are likely to lead to frustration on the part of providers, as they perceive that formulary decisions are made for economic rather than clinical reasons. Moreover, these types of decisions necessarily involve prescribers as the agents of change (e.g., for a therapeutic switch), thereby increasing their workload.

The fact that prescribers often must adhere to multiple conflicting formulary policies from multiple payers adds to the challenges they face. Therefore, it should not be surprising if prescribers regard dealing with various sets of formularies or drug lists and prescription procedures as an onerous task that is time-consuming and cumbersome. *Thus, although TRICARE does not currently have a formulary or preferred drug list, prescribers' experiences with other pharmacy benefits packages and health plans may not only influence the type of prescriptions they write for TRICARE patients but will also form the basis for how they initially perceive and interact with the UF once it is implemented. Prescribers may have negative perceptions of the UF for reasons totally unrelated to any problems inherent in the formulary itself.*

The National Mail Order Pharmacy

In 1998, in response to cost concerns, the DoD carved away the mail-order dispensing of drugs from TRICARE contracts and replaced it with a single NMOP. The DoD P&T committee determines which drugs are available through the NMOP and the rules governing the dispensing of those drugs, such as the rules that define which drugs require prior authorization before being dispensed.

The NMOP program is currently administered and managed through a contract with Merck-Medco Managed Care. Beneficiaries can obtain a 90-day supply of drugs (or a 30-day supply for controlled medications including narcotics) for a lower co-payment than the co-payment to fill prescriptions at retail pharmacies. In addition, refillable prescriptions initially filled through the NMOP can be obtained relatively quickly by ordering through the mail, by telephone, or over the Internet. The NMOP prescriptions are subject to safety review and undergo mandatory generic substitution.[8]

---

[8]The NMOP program is described in greater detail at http://www.tricare.osd.mil/pharmacy/nmop.cfm.

Concerns About the Current System

The DoD's management of its three prescription programs has been the subject of scrutiny by the GAO (U.S. General Accounting Office, 1998 and 1999a) acting at the behest of Congress. The GAO evaluations noted a number of concerns in several areas.

The first of these concerns arose from the lack of pharmacy data from TRICARE contractors and the overall lack of integration between medical records and pharmacy data. However, with the implementation of the Pharmacy Benefit Redesign Program in 2001 and more specifically the implementation of the PDTS in 2001 across all points of service, this concern has been largely addressed. The PDTS provides for a comprehensive and coordinated tracking system that enables providers to capture potential drug-drug interactions and monitor safety issues.

A second concern arose from inconsistencies in the drug benefit. Until April 1, 2001, access rules and cost sharing for pharmaceuticals schedules differed across eight classes of beneficiaries: active duty (in TRICARE Prime), active duty family member in TRICARE Prime, active duty family member in TRICARE Extra or Standard, retirees and dependents under age 65 in TRICARE Prime, retirees and dependents under age 65 in TRICARE Extra or Standard, Medicare-eligible retirees, Medicare-eligible retirees with BRAC benefits, and Medicare-eligible retirees in TRICARE Senior Prime. The three pharmacy programs and eight beneficiary classes resulted in 24 different drug benefit schemes (see U.S. General Accounting Office, 1998, Table 3.1). Again, with the implementation of the new co-payment structure in April 2001, the eight classes of beneficiaries were eliminated and replaced with a streamlined co-pay structure based on the formulary status of the drug rather than the status of the beneficiary.

A third concern was that co-payments were largely unrelated to what the DoD pays to acquire the medication; thus, co-pays provided little incentive for beneficiaries to seek out dispensing locations with the lowest costs to the DoD, with the exception of the incentives for using network versus non-network retail pharmacies. Moreover, for many beneficiary types, uniform co-payment schedules, ranging from five to nine dollars, did not discourage their purchasing prescriptions for more expensive alternatives within a drug class. Providers and patients had little incentive to switch to less-expensive agents within a drug class, as might occur within the statin or angiotensin converting enzyme inhibitor drug classes, when the co-payment structure for preferred and non-preferred drugs was similar. The new UF program and the three-tier co-pay structure, discussed in the next section, seek to address this issue.

The Structure of the Uniform Formulary Program

As noted in Chapter 1, the NDAA for FY 2000 requires the DoD to integrate its pharmacy programs with the UF and directs the DoD to develop additional systems to administer drug benefits (e.g., the PDTS).[9] The UF will be an open formulary that is intended to include the entire range of generic and brand-name drugs required to treat DoD beneficiaries. Although the details of the UF are still in the rule-making/comment stage as of this writing, in the following sections we include an overview of the proposed rule as published in the *Federal Register* ("Civilian Health and Medical Program ...," 2002). The proposed rule is subject to change during the comment period and will not be considered final until it is published in the *Federal Register*. Following the publication of the final rule, the DoD P&T committee will determine the contents of the UF, and a Beneficiary Advisory Panel will be given the opportunity to voice their comments to the director of the TRICARE program before the UF is implemented within the MHS.

Access to and Availability of Pharmaceuticals

In accordance with the proposed UF rule and the NDAA FY 2000 statute, the UF "shall assure the availability of pharmaceutical agents in the complete range of therapeutic classes authorized under the TRICARE prescription benefit."

According to the proposed UF rule, pharmaceutical agents in each therapeutic class will be selected for inclusion in the UF based on their relative clinical effectiveness and cost effectiveness. If an agent is determined to not have a significant, clinically meaningful therapeutic advantage compared with other drugs included on the UF, or if it is determined to be not cost effective relative to other UF drugs, it may be classified as a non-formulary agent. Agents used exclusively for medical conditions that are excluded from the TRICARE benefit by statute or by regulation will not be considered for inclusion in the UF.

All pharmaceutical agents included on the UF shall be available through the MTF pharmacies, and the availability shall be consistent with the scope of practice at such facilities. The BCF that is currently in place will become a subset of the UF and will continue to be a mandatory component of all MTF pharmacy formularies.

---

[9]Information on the structure of the UF and coverage decisionmaking is from a DoD report to Congress on the subject in December 2000; personal communications with Colonel William Davies, director, DoD Pharmacy Benefits Program, September 8, 2000, and "Civilian Health and Medical Program . . .," (2002), pp. 17948–17954.

The proposed rule also sets forth procedures to determine which agents will be included in the UF and which will require prior authorization before they are dispensed, and to determine generic drug classification, availability of non-formulary medications to members of the uniformed services and eligible covered beneficiaries, and reduction of co-payments for cases of clinical necessity.

Cost Sharing and the Three-Tier Co-Payment Structure

The FY 2000 NDAA legislation allows the DoD to designate a three-tier co-payment price structure based on the classification of the prescribed drugs: (1) generic drugs (with the least-expensive co-payment); (2) formulary or preferred drugs (with the next-least-expensive co-payment); and (3) non-formulary or non-preferred drugs (with the most-expensive co-payment).

Active duty members currently do not pay a cost share and will continue not to do so. Cost sharing for all other beneficiaries will be based upon the pharmaceutical agent's classification in the UF (i.e., generic, formulary, or non-formulary) and the point of service (i.e., MTF, retail network pharmacy, retail non-network pharmacy, or the NMOP) from which the agent is acquired. The co-pay structure, organized by point of service, is outlined in Table 2.2.

The Uniform Formulary Versus the Current System

The UF program will represent a major shift for the purchased-care system, in which formularies currently are open and offer few opportunities for the DoD to manage drug benefit costs. For the direct-care system (i.e., drugs dispensed at the MTF), the proposed UF will provide an expanded BCF and allow local MTF P&T committees to continue to make additions based on the scope of care. For the NMOP (for prescriptions written by either a direct-care provider or purchased-care provider), the UF will make non-formulary medications available at the third-tier co-pay. In the retail network pharmacies (again, for prescriptions written by either a direct- or purchased-care provider), the UF makes the non-formulary medications accessible at the third tier co-pay for a 90-day supply.

Table 2.2

Proposed Three-Tier Co-Payment Structure

	MTF	Network Retail	NMOP	Non-Network Retail
		Point of Service		
Tier 1: Generic brands	No cost	$3 per prescription for 30-day supply	$3 per prescription for a 90-day supply	$9 or 20% (whichever is greater) per prescription for a 30-day supply
Tier 2: Formulary proprietary brands	No cost	$9 per prescription for a 30-day supply	$9 per prescription for a 90-day supply	$9 or 20% (the greater of the two) per prescription for a 30-day supply; deductibles and point of service penalties also apply
Tier 3: Non-formulary, non-preferred brands	Not available unless prescribed by an MTF provider and approved through special order process	$22 per prescription for a 30-day supply	$22 per prescription for a 90-day supply	$22 or 20% (the greater of the two) per prescription for a 30-day supply; deductibles and point of service penalties also apply

Development and Maintenance of the Uniform Formulary

The NDAA requires the DoD P&T committee to develop and maintain the UF. The committee will consist of government and non-government clinical staff. Its primary function will be to define the UF, excluding drugs only if they do not have a "significant, clinically meaningful" therapeutic advantage over other included drugs in terms of safety, effectiveness, or clinical outcomes.

The UF development will occur in six stages:

1. Identification of the universe of covered therapeutic classes.

2. Identification of candidate drugs in each class.

3. Evaluation of drugs within each class to determine their relative safety and clinical efficacy.

4. Consideration of the relative costs of drugs in a particular class in relation to safety and clinical efficacy to determine their relative cost-effectiveness.

5. Identification of candidates for exclusion from the UF on the basis of Steps 3 and 4.

6. Submission of recommendations to the Uniform Formulary Beneficiary Advisory Panel for review and comment.

Surveys to Assess the Impact of the Uniform Formulary on Prescribers

To assess prescribers' perspectives on the perceived impact of the UF within the Military Health System, the TMA asked RAND to conduct a confidential survey of TRICARE prescribers who practice in MTFs or within network facilities following implementation of the UF. RAND will administer the post-implementation survey of MHS prescribers to assess the impact of the UF on prescribers in terms of their workload, sense of autonomy, patient access, and patient relationships, and to assess their perceptions of the uniform formulary's impact on the quality and cost effectiveness of care.

To establish a baseline for a better understanding of prescribers' current prescribing behavior and their knowledge of and attitudes about formularies and formulary management systems, RAND conducted a pre-UF (i.e., baseline) survey in 2001. The following chapters outline the methods and results of that baseline survey effort.

3. Survey and Sample Design

In fall 2000, 700 direct-care providers within MTFs and 600 purchased-care providers at network facilities were sampled using data obtained from claims records. In this chapter, we discuss the development of the survey questionnaire and our sampling strategy and design.

Questionnaire Development

Separate baseline (i.e., pre-UF) questionnaires were developed for each of the two sample populations—direct-care prescribers and purchased-care prescribers. Questionnaire development for both surveys began in September 2000.

The first steps in developing the questionnaire were to identify the domains that would be examined in the survey and then to locate appropriate reference materials. The reference materials included two instruments developed by the VA Pharmacy Benefits Management Strategic Healthcare Group and RAND for the Survey of Pharmacy Benefits of VA providers in 2000. We also reviewed the questionnaire used in the VA Formulary Study conducted by the U.S. General Accounting Office in 2000. Both the direct-care and purchased-care questionnaires were developed concurrently through the pilot-testing phase and were designed to collect the same domains of information.

Direct-Care Prescribers' Questionnaire

The draft survey instrument for direct-care prescribers was reviewed by four MTF physicians/researchers[1] in early December 2000. Input was received from three of these individuals, and various formatting and wording changes were made in response to the reviewers' comments. A pilot test of the instrument was planned, but, given logistical and timing issues, we were unable to conduct this pilot test before the instrument had to be fielded in spring 2001 (see Chapter 4 for an explanation of why fielding needed to occur in the spring.) However, input was obtained from various TMA staff members and incorporated in the final version of the questionnaire.

---

[1]The physicians/researchers are colleagues of Peter Glassman, the principal investigator of this study.

26

The baseline questionnaire, which was divided into four sections (see Table 3.1), was designed to elicit information regarding the respondent's experience as a prescriber within an MTF, with particular attention to potential difficulties encountered with the current MTF formulary system. The first three sections of the baseline questionnaire collected information regarding the prescriber's experiences with and opinions about previous formularies (prior to the implementation of a new formulary system). The last section of the questionnaire collected background information on the respondent (e.g., education, age, employment status, and practice characteristics). A copy of the final survey can be found in Appendix A.

Purchased-Care Prescribers' Questionnaire

The draft survey instrument for purchased-care (or "network") prescribers was sent for review to eight civilian physicians/researchers[2] in early January 2001. Input was received from four of these individuals, and various formatting and wording changes were made in response to the reviewers' comments. A pilot test of the revised instrument was conducted in early April 2001. Surveys were distributed to a convenience sample of nine prescribers in the San Antonio area (seven in the TRICARE Network and two who were not in Network but who had submitted claims on behalf of TRICARE patients). Of the nine recipients, seven completed and returned the surveys. Minor changes were made to the instrument based on their responses. More significant changes were made based on input obtained from various TMA staff members.

The baseline network questionnaire was designed to elicit information regarding respondents' experiences as prescribers in general, with particular attention to issues related to TRICARE patients. The questionnaire collected baseline information regarding prescribers' exposure to, experience with, and opinion of formulary systems and preferred-drug-list systems prior to the implementation of the new formulary system. Information on each respondent's background and scope of practice (e.g., education, age, employment status, and practice characteristics) was also collected. The questionnaire was divided into five sections (see Table 3.2). A copy of the final survey can be found in Appendix B.

Both the direct-care and purchased-care questionnaires, and the design and implementation methods, were reviewed and approved by RAND's Human Subjects Protection Committee. In addition, the purchased-care questionnaire

[2]The physicians/researchers are colleagues of Peter Glassman.

Table 3.1

Sections of Direct-Care Prescribers' Questionnaire

Section	Topic
1	Prescribing patterns/behaviors and experiences with the formulary system
2	Opinions regarding patient behaviors and prescription drugs (including DTC advertisement) and the MTF formulary content and procedures
3	Opinions regarding the MTF P&T committee and about how to improve the formulary system
4	Background and scope of practice information

Table 3.2

Sections of Purchased-Care Prescribers' Questionnaire

Section	Topic
1	Prescribing patterns/behaviors and experiences with formulary systems
2	Opinions regarding P&T committees and about how to improve the formulary system
3	Opinions regarding DTC advertisement of prescription drugs
4	Medical practice as it relates to TRICARE patients
5	Background and scope of practice information

and data collection were submitted for Office of Management and Budget (OMB) review and approval. OMB approval of this instrument was received in June 2001 (OMB Approval 0720-0024). The direct-care questionnaire did not require OMB approval because it is aimed at active duty military or government employees working in government-owned MTFs, and such employees are excluded from OMB review.

Sampling Strategy

Section 701 of the NDAA for FY 2000 specifically required that the survey include MTF prescribers and non-MTF prescribers under TRICARE contracts. The legislation also defined prescribers as "physicians, physician assistants, and nurse practitioners." Our first goal was to understand the characteristics of the universe of MHS prescribers. To achieve this goal, we consulted with our sponsor to evaluate the availability of existing information on prescribers, including information regarding practice setting, provider type, and specialty area.

To conduct this study within the scope of the legislation and available project resources, the sponsor and RAND study team agreed that the survey would target the subgroups of prescribers most likely to be affected by the new UF. This group included those who see large numbers of outpatients and those who prescribe a wide range of therapeutic classes of drugs. We were concerned mostly with primary-care providers because they represented the majority of MHS providers; however, we also included specialists in our sample population. Because the current formulary structures and systems affect MHS prescribers within MTFs differently than they affect prescribers contracted through TRICARE networks, these groups are treated as two distinct samples. While the principles applied to the sampling strategy were similar, the sampling frame files were created and manipulated differently. Our goal was to make the two samples as comparable as possible, yet at the same time representative of the differences between the two distinct systems.

A ready-made list of MHS prescribers in these systems was not available. Instead, relevant information was drawn from ambulatory visit records (e.g., administrative data) and provider records. Our methods for identifying these samples are described next. Additional details on how the sampling frame files were constructed can be obtained from the authors or the study sponsor (see the preface for contact information).

Direct-Care Prescribers' Sample Design

For purposes of creating the direct-care sampling frame, the DoD provided an Excel file containing data merged from the Standard Ambulatory Data Record (SADR) and the Composite Health Care System (CHCS) provider file. This file was created using SADRs from September 2000 through November 2000 to generate "visit counts" by treatment site and provider identification (ID) number. These data were linked by provider ID with information from the July 2001 (representing Time 1 [T1]) extract from the CHCS provider files.

The T1 file is a compilation of provider data pulled from all MTFs. Thus, for purposes of this effort, the population of MTF prescribers is defined as providers within MTFs who had provider data contained in the July T1 file and who had at least one patient appointment (as recorded in SADR data) any time between September 1, 2000, and November 30, 2000. The resulting file contained 16,383 records with the provider names and MTF codes, provider specialty code, and number of appointments over the three-month period. In the remainder of this section, this file is referred to as the "SADR file."

The prescriber's full name (first name, last name, and middle initial) was used as an identifying variable because this variable had the most unique values, and the file contained no other unique identifier. In addition, the sampling frame did not contain data to measure prescribing frequency directly, but the file did include a variable that measured the number of appointments during a three-month period. The number of appointments varied widely across all groups of providers in all settings from a low of 1 to more than 1,500. Low values may represent prescribers who were away on deployments for part of the sampling period and high values may represent assignment of responsibility to clinic supervisors for patients who were actually seen by clinic staff or residents. To avoid these unusual cases, prescribers with fewer than 120 appointments (2 per day for 60 days) or more than 1,440 (roughly 24 appointments lasting 20 minutes each per day for 60 days) were dropped (the number dropped equaled 2,138).

To define the specialty populations of interest, the range of provider specialties within each of the sampling frame files was reviewed. However, the SADR file contained more-detailed specialty information than the sampling frame file for the purchased-care providers. Therefore, to make the two provider surveys comparable, only those specialty types most likely to have large outpatient caseloads and specialty definitions roughly parallel with the provider types in the purchased-care sample were included. As a result, many prescribers who were "residents" and "consultants" and many types of subspecialties that did not appear in the purchased-care file (e.g., oncologists) were dropped (the number dropped equaled 10,954). After dropping records with missing MTF information (n = 40), missing names (n = 1,277), individuals practicing off site (n = 1,892), extreme values for appointment frequency (n = 2,138), duplicate names (n = 82), and ineligible specialties (n = 10,954), 3,513 individuals remained in the sampling frame who were eligible for inclusion in the sample. To assure adequate representation of specialists and prescribers assigned to small MTFs (who would otherwise be underrepresented for the purposes of statistical analysis), a stratification strategy was employed. Based on an a priori understanding of important analytic variables, the sample was stratified by the size of the MTF and prescriber specialty. Power calculations suggested that 60 sample members per strata would be sufficient to detect a true difference of at least 10 percent across specialty and MTF size categories at conventional levels of significance (alpha = 0.05). Thus, it was important to keep the number of categories within each stratum small, in light of sample size limitations of 600 in each of the two sectors.

Prescribers who met our inclusion criteria (as stated earlier) were grouped into four categories: (1) General practitioners (primary care); (2) obstetricians/gynecologists and pediatricians; (3) specialists and subspecialists; and 4) non-M.D. (non-physician) prescribers (see Table 3.3).[3]

The number of prescribers working in any clinic or installation affiliated with the MTF, but not necessarily within the physical MTF facility, was used as a measure

---

[3]Although obstetricians/gynecologists and pediatricians were combined for the purpose of sampling, they were analyzed as separate provider groups.

Table 3.3

Specialty Types Included in Direct-Care and Purchased-Care Samples

Provider Type	Direct-Care Sample	Purchased-Care Sample
General practitioners	Family practice physician Family practice physician/ primary care General medical officer General medicine practitioner Geriatrician Gerontologist/geriatric physician Internal medicine practitioner Internist	Family practice physician General practice physician Geriatric physician Internist Nurse practitioner Physician's assistant
Obstetricians/ gynecologists	Gynecologist Obstetrician Obstetrician/gynecologist	Obstetrician/gynecologist
Specialists/ Subspecialists	Allergist Allergist, pediatric Cardiologist Cardiologist, pediatric Dermatologist Dermatologist, pediatric Dermatology resident Endocrinologist Gastroenterologist Nephrologist Neurologist, pediatric Obstetrician/gynecologist Oncologist, obstetrical and gynecological Pediatric nephrologist Pediatric neurologist Pulmonary disease physician Pulmonary disease physician, pediatric	Allergist Cardiovascular physician Dermatologist Endocrinologist Gastroenterologist Nephrologist Neurologist Pulmonary disease physician
Pediatricians	Adolescent medicine practitioner Pediatrician Physician, pediatrics	Pediatrician
Non-M.D. prescribers	Clinical nurse, entry-level Nurse practitioner Obstetrics/gynecology nurse practitioner Pediatric nurse practitioner Physician assistant Primary care nurse practitioner, entry-level Primary care nurse practitioner, qualified	Sample is included with General practitioners

of MTF size. We believe this number better captures administrative complexity and is therefore more closely related to formulary processes and procedures than the number of individuals practicing solely at the "parent" MTF. For purposes of stratification, we created a three-level variable for MTF size: "small" is 100 or fewer prescribers, "medium" is 101 to 500 providers, and "large" is 501 or more.

For several reasons, after creating our MTF size variable, we dropped prescribers not practicing at the "parent" MTF. First, we had less confidence in the availability and validity of address information on "satellite clinics" than there was on parent MTFs. Second, because it is unclear exactly what activities take place at the non-parent installations, it is not possible to be confident that all survey questions were relevant to each respondent. For example, some off-site installations may have much more restricted formularies due the lack of physical space or appropriate storage facilities (e.g., adequate and reliable refrigeration).

A set of sampling weights was created such that a stratified random sample would contain at least 60 individuals in each category of our two stratification variables (MTF size and provider type). This was done under the assumption that 50 percent of the sample would respond (thus, 50 percent is our low-end response rate assumption). Because of the inclusion criteria stated earlier, the non-physician category had only 53 members and could be combined with general practitioners if the number of returned surveys was too small to support treating non-M.D. prescribers as a separate group in our statistical analysis. The "target" sample proportions are such that 33 percent of the sample were intended to come from small MTFs, 33 percent from medium MTFs, and 33 percent from large MTFs. Likewise, 30 percent were intended to be general practitioners, 30 percent either obstetricians/gynecologists or pediatricians, 30 percent subspecialists, and 10 percent would be non-physician prescribers. Table 3.4 shows the actual population and sample proportions in each stratum.

Purchased-Care Prescribers' Sample Design

The method used to draw the purchased-care sample was similar to the method used to draw the sample from the direct-care system. For purposes of creating a sampling frame, we used a file that contained information that resulted from a merger of data from CHAMPUS/TRICARE Health Care Service Records (HCSRs)[4] with data from the CHAMPUS/TRICARE Health Care Provider Records (HCPRs) maintained by TMA in Aurora, Colorado.

---

[4]These are claims data with care-end dates in September and October 2000.

32

Table 3.4

Population and Sample Proportions by MTF Size and Provider Type for Direct-Care Prescribers' Sample

| Provider | Population Proportions | | | | Sample Proportions | | | |
| | MTF Size | | | | MTF Size | | | |
Type	Small	Medium	Large	Total	Small	Medium	Large	Total
General practitioners	455	666	274	1,395	66	63	49	178
Percentage of total (within the row)	32.62	47.74	19.64	100.00	37.08	35.39	27.53	100.00
Percentage of total (within the column)	46.52	39.60	32.12	39.71	45.83	33.16	18.42	29.67
Obstetri-cians/gyne-cologists and pediatricians	172	363	183	718	48	59	71	178
Percentage of total (within the row)	23.96	50.56	25.49	100.00	26.97	33.15	39.89	100.00
Percentage of total (within the column)	17.59	21.58	21.45	20.44	33.33	31.05	26.69	29.67
Subspecialists	19	200	272	491	9	47	135	191
Percentage of total (within the row)	3.87	40.73	55.40	100.00	4.71	24.61	70.68	100.00
Percentage of total (within the column)	1.94	11.89	31.89	13.98	6.25	24.74	50.75	31.83
Non-M.D. prescribers	332	453	124	909	21	21	11	53
Percentage of total (within the row)	36.52	49.83	13.64	100.00	39.62	39.62	20.75	100.00
Percentage of total (within the column)	33.95	26.93	14.54	25.88	14.58	11.05	4.14	8.83
Total	978	1682	853	3,513	144	190	266	600
Percentage of total (within the row)	27.84	47.88	24.28	100.00	24.00	31.67	44.33	100.00
Percentage of total (within the column)	100.00	100.00	100.00	100.00	100.00	100.00	100.00	100.00

Prior to merging the claims data information with the provider data, TMA provided RAND with a file for manipulation and cleaning that contained claims data extracted from the HCSRs. Following the manipulation, the file was returned to TMA for extraction of additional information on providers identified by RAND. This step was done to narrow the list of individuals for whom contact information was needed. The following section describes the sampling strategy applied during the manipulation of the first file provided by TMA.

The file based on the HCSRs contained 200,258 provider numbers for all clinicians who filed claims for reimbursement in the purchased-care system during September and October 2000 (these providers define the survey population). Providers in this file were uniquely identified through a combination of their provider number, "sub ID," and zip code. Because the file was drawn from claims data, it contained very little information about the providers other than their specialty and the zip code in which they provided care. The file also contained fields related to the MHS region from which the patients originated. Because the extent to which these fields accurately characterize the location of providers is not known, they were not used for sampling. The file contained a field for the number of claims filed and the amount that TMA paid to the provider over a two-month period.

Like the SADR data, the HCSR data did not contain a measure of prescribing frequency. Therefore, we concluded that the most reliable variable in the data was the number of claims in the two-month period. While claims and visits do not directly coincide because some visits generate multiple claims, we believed that the number of claims was a better measure of TRICARE visit frequency than the amount paid. Overall, the providers included in the file did not appear to submit HCSR claims very frequently. For example, more than 70 percent of the sample filed four or fewer claims during the two-month period.

Two types of providers were dropped from the sampling frame:

- To improve our ability to generalize from our analyses, we dropped providers with multiple specialties because there was no information in the database that enabled us to identify a primary specialty (n = 1,655).

- To conserve scarce project resources, providers with multiple zip codes were also dropped (n = 11,673). The data contained multiple zip codes because providers render care in more than one location. However, the data contained no information to indicate which was the primary location. Consultation with our sponsor suggested that it was not possible to obtain information that would allow us to select the best mailing address among multiple zip codes. Because the median number of claims in the sample was so small (fewer than two), this variable was not useful for inferring which zip code best corresponded to the primary practice location. Exploratory analysis suggested that dropping providers with multiple zip codes had little, if any, impact on the distribution of specialties or claim intensity in the final sample.

After dropping the records of prescribers with multiple specialties (n = 1,665), those with multiple zip codes (n = 11,673), and subspecialists who did not see large numbers of outpatients (n = 13,218), 131,602 records remained that met our inclusion criteria.

Again, based on an a priori understanding of important analytic variables, claim intensity (as a proxy measure for visit frequency) and provider specialty were chosen as stratification variables. To represent specialists and low- and medium-intensity claiming prescribers, the sample was stratified based on prescriber specialty type and claims intensity. Physicians who met our inclusion criteria were classified into three specialty groups: (1) general practitioners, (2) obstetricians/gynecologists and pediatricians, and (3) specialists. Although the overall goal was to draw the direct-care and purchased-care samples with roughly comparable specialty definitions, the specialty categorization in the purchased-care sample was somewhat different from that used in the direct-care sample. The purchased-care sample contained less-detailed specialty information, and non-physician prescribers constituted a smaller proportion of the sample (less than 2 percent versus 26 percent in the direct-care sample).

Because civilian non-physician providers rarely submit claims on their own behalf, we suspected that the non-physician prescribers who filed HCSR claims did not represent the general population of non-physician prescribers in the purchased-care system very well. For this reason, a unique specialty category for non-physician providers was not created. Instead, they were included in the "general practitioner" category. A three-level measure of claims intensity was also created: providers who filed 10 or more claims were classified "low intensity," those who filed 11 to 40 claims were classified "middle intensity," and those who filed more than 40 claims were "high intensity" providers.

To insure at least 60 respondents in each category with a 50-percent response rate, a set of sampling weights was created such that a stratified random sample would contain prescribers from each of the strata in roughly equal proportions. The "target" sample proportions were such that 33 percent of the sample would come from each prescriber specialty category, and 33 percent of the sample would come from each level of the three claims-intensity levels. Table 3.5 shows the sample proportions in each stratum.

Table 3.5

Population and Sample Proportions by Claims Intensity and Provider Type for Purchased-Care Sample

Provider Type	Population Proportions Claims Intensity				Sample Proportions Claims Intensity			
	Low	Medium	High	Total	Low	Medium	High	Total
General practitioners	76,596	6,138	1,317	84,051	69	66	73	208
Percentage of total (within the row)	91.13	7.30	1.57	100.00	33.17	31.73	35.10	100.00
Percentage of total (within the column)	64.00	62.62	62.39	63.87	34.67	34.74	34.60	34.67
Obstetricians/gynecologists and pediatricians	22,477	1,927	459	24,863	66	53	77	196
Percentage of total (within the row)	90.40	7.75	1.85	100.00	33.67	27.04	39.29	100.00
Percentage of total (within the column)	18.78	19.66	21.74	18.89	33.17	27.89	36.49	32.67
Specialists	20,616	1,737	335	22,688	64	71	61	196
Percentage of total (within the row)	90.87	7.66	1.48	100.00	32.65	36.22	31.12	100.00
Percentage of total (within the column)	17.22	17.72	15.87	17.24	32.16	37.37	28.91	32.67
Total	119,689	9,802	2,111	131,602	199	190	211	600
Percentage of total (within the row)	90.95	7.45	1.60	100.00	33.17	31.67	35.17	100.00
Percentage of total (within the column)	100.00	100.00	100.00	100.00	100.00	100.00	100.00	100.00

4. Data Collection and Response Analysis

Data Collection for Direct-Care Prescribers

Data collection efforts for the direct-care prescribers' survey began in early April 2001 and were completed by the end of July 2001. Given that the survey sample had been identified using TMA administrative data from 2000, it was critical that the survey fielding be completed by July 2001 to minimize the number of respondents who would no longer be at the MTF at which they were originally sampled. During the planning phase of the project, it came to our attention that most transfers occur during the summer period and that in a one-year time period, the transfer rate for MTF medical personnel can be as high as 30 percent.

During the first mailing, a study packet was sent via U.S. mail to 600 direct-care prescribers (Appendix A reproduces the contents of the packet). The study packet included an introductory letter on RAND letterhead signed by one of the principal investigators, a hard copy of the questionnaire, and a postage-paid return envelope for returning the completed questionnaire. The letter included a toll-free number for respondents to call with questions or concerns. The study packet was sent to the mailing address of the MTF to which the respondent was known to be assigned at the time the sample was drawn.

After two weeks, a reminder letter was sent via U.S. mail to all 600 sampled prescribers. After another three weeks (by early May 2001), a second mailing was sent to all non-responders to the first mailing (n = 368). This mailing excluded providers for whom the first study packet or the reminder letter was returned undelivered without a usable forwarding address. The study packet again included a letter signed by one of the principal investigators, a hard copy of the questionnaire, and a postage-paid return envelope for returning the completed questionnaire. In addition, given an undeliverable rate of 10 percent from the first mailing, 100 new cases were sampled and mailed the questionnaire for the first time during this second mailing wave.

Reminder phone calls began in late May 2001 (four weeks after the second mailing wave) and lasted until late July. These calls targeted all active cases (i.e., all cases of those who had not yet returned a completed survey but who had not actively refused or who had not been determined to be no longer eligible to participate). For the majority of active cases, these calls were designed to determine if the respondent had received the questionnaire and, if so, to urge the respondent to complete the survey. However, for the cases with study packets returned undelivered, these calls were used to determine if the respondent was in fact no longer at the MTF to which the packet had been sent, or whether we simply did not have the correct address within that MTF to reach the respondent (see Appendix A for a sample of our calling script). By the end of the reminder call phase of the survey, all cases whose study packet had been returned undelivered were determined to be either no longer eligible to participate or to need a re-mail to a revised address within the MTF to which we originally sent the study packet.

During the reminder phone call phase of the survey, we became aware that all 35 cases originally thought to be in one particular MTF were in fact not there. (TMA had provided the wrong address for that MTF.) In lieu of trying to determine the correct MTF and address for these 35 cases, they were replaced with 35 new randomly selected cases from MTFs of the same size. The study packet was mailed to these replacement cases in mid-June 2001.

A third and final mailing wave was done by the middle of July to all active cases (n = 257). As with previous mailings, this mailing included a cover letter (see Appendix A), a copy of the questionnaire, and a postage-paid return envelope. However, given that we needed to complete the fielding of the survey before the end of July, this packet was sent via FedEx. This shipment method delivered the packet to the potential respondent quickly and gave the study packet a sense of urgency, thus potentially influencing the individual to review its contents and respond promptly.

Data Collection for Purchased-Care Prescribers

Data collection efforts for the purchased-care prescribers' survey began in mid-July 2001 and were completed by the beginning of November 2001.

During the first mailing, study packets were sent via U.S. mail to 600 purchased-care prescribers (the packet is reproduced in Appendix B). The study packet included an introductory letter on RAND letterhead that was signed by one of the principal investigators, a hard copy of the questionnaire, and a postage-paid return envelope for returning the completed questionnaire. The letter included a toll-free number for respondents to call with questions or concerns. The study packet was sent to the office mailing address, which we obtained when the sample was drawn using TMA administrative data from 2000.

Given that the survey sample had been identified using TMA administrative data from 2000 and that close to 5 percent of study packets were being returned as undeliverable, the decision was made to begin the reminder phone call phase shortly after the first mailing (in lieu of sending a reminder letter). We made these phone calls between follow-up mailings starting the last week of July 2001 through the beginning of October. These calls targeted all active cases (i.e., all cases of those who had not yet returned a completed survey but who had not actively refused or who had not been determined to no be longer eligible to participate). For the majority of active cases, these calls were designed to determine if the respondent had received the questionnaire and, if so, to urge the respondent to complete the survey. However, these calls also served to determine if the respondent had a new address (see Appendix B for a sample of our calling script). By the end of the reminder call phase of the survey, all cases whose study packet had been returned as undeliverable were determined either to be no longer eligible to participate or to need a re-mail to a revised address if the address was within 25 miles of the original address to which the study packet was sent.

By mid-August (one month after the first mailing), a second study packet was mailed to all active cases (n = 502), which again included a letter signed by one of the principal investigators (see Appendix B), a hard copy of the questionnaire, and a postage-paid return envelope for returning the completed questionnaire. Given the low response rate to the first mailing wave, the decision was made to send the second mailing via FedEx. As with the MTF sample, the hope was that this shipment method would give the study packet a sense of urgency, thereby increasing the likelihood that the individual would review its contents and respond promptly.

A third and final mailing wave was done in late September 2001 to all active cases (n = 320). As with the previous mailings, a copy of the questionnaire and a postage-paid return envelope was sent. As was done with the second mailing, the third mailing was sent via FedEx. However, instead of a cover letter, we included a flyer-type insert (see Appendix B) on yellow paper hoping that the insert would grab the attention of the person opening the FedEx envelope.

By the end of the reminder phone call phase (at the beginning of October), fewer than 35 percent of potential participants had returned a completed survey. As a final attempt to boost the response rate, a reminder fax (see Appendix B) was sent at the beginning of November to all active cases for whom we were able to obtain a fax number (n = 260).

Data collection for both surveys was closed on December 3, 2001, and all completed surveys were edited and entered by December 14, 2001. Data entry was completed in December 2001, and the files were 100 percent verified (i.e., with double-data entry).

Survey Response Status and Participation Rates

Table 4.1 provides a breakdown of response status and rates for both samples.

Direct-care prescribers were considered "Ineligible" if they were no longer at the MTF to which they were assigned when the sampling frame was identified (they were designated "Out of Area"), or if they indicated that they do not treat patients or do not have prescribing privileges (they were designated "Not Qualified"). Purchased-care prescribers were considered "Ineligible" if their new address was more than 25 miles from the address to which the study packet was originally mailed ("Out of Area"), or if they indicated that they are not prescribers, do not treat outpatients, or have never treated TRICARE patients "Not Qualified").

"Eligible" respondents were broken down into three categories: (1) "Active Non-Respondent" cases were those for whom the survey was not returned completed by the respondent nor was it returned as undeliverable by the mailing service; (2) "Refused to Participate" were cases who indicated that they are not interested in participating or are too busy to participate; and (3) "Eligible Respondents" were those who did not fall into either of the first two categories.

The response rate is calculated by dividing the number of eligible respondents who returned a completed survey (whether partially or entirely filled out) by the total number of eligible respondents. The final response rate for the direct-care prescribers' survey was 69 percent, and the response rate for the purchased-care prescribers' survey was 38 percent.

Analysis of Non-Response

To assess potential sources of bias, we conducted two analyses—one for each of the two samples—to detect systematic differences between respondents and non-respondents on the basis of characteristics of prescribers contained in the sampling frame. The analysis of non-response is inherently limited because we are not able to detect differences between responders and non-responders that are not measured by the information in the sampling frames.

Table 4.1

Final Survey Participation and Response Rates

	Direct-Care Prescribers		Purchased-Care Prescribers	
Total Sample	N = 700		N = 600	
	N	% of Total Sample	N	% of Total Sample
Total Ineligible Cases	134	19	43	7
Out of area	115	16	32	5
Not qualified	19	3	11	2
	N	% of Eligible Sample	N	% of Eligible Sample[a]
Total Eligible Cases	566	100	557	100
Active non-respondent	157	28	250	44
Refused to participate	20	3	97	17
Eligible respondents	389	69	210	38

[a]Does not add to 100% due to rounding.

Direct-Care Prescribers

We estimated a binomial logit model of completion of the direct-care survey among 548 eligible respondents with complete data as a function of (1) visits in a two-month period; (2) indicators of specialty type (primary-care physician, obstetrician/gynecologist, pediatrician, other specialist, physician's assistant, or advanced practice nurse); (3) indicators of MTF size (small, medium, or large); and (4) gender. Binomial logit coefficients and odds ratios are reported in Table C.1 in Appendix C.

Being female ($p < 0.10$) and being a non-physician prescriber ($p < 0.05$) were the only statistically significant predictors of survey response. Eligible females were 50 percent more likely to respond to the survey than their male counterparts, and non-physician prescribers were two and a half times more likely to respond than were physicians. All other characteristics were insignificant.

Purchased-Care Prescribers

We estimated a binomial logit model of completion of the purchased-care survey among 468 eligible respondents, with complete data being a function of (1) the number of claims submitted in a two-month period; (2) indicators of specialty type (primary-care physician, obstetrician/gynecologist, pediatrician, other specialist); (3) indicators of practice location within an MTF catchment area; (4) indicators of a TRICARE managed-care support contract operating in the

42

prescribers' health care service region; and (5) the amount paid by TRICARE for the care it provided in a two-month period. Binomial logit coefficients and odds ratios are reported in Table D.2 in Appendix D.

Practicing in an MTF catchment area ($p < 0.05$) and being an obstetrician/ gynecologist ($p < 0.10$) were statistically significant predictors of survey response. Eligible respondents practicing inside MTF catchment areas were roughly 60 percent more likely to respond than those practicing outside MTF catchment areas, and obstetrician/gynecologists were almost twice as likely as primary-care physicians to respond. All other characteristics were insignificant.

5. Summary of Findings

In this chapter, we present our findings in a series of charts and tables summarizing the distribution of survey responses. As we discussed earlier, due to distinct differences in the direct-care and purchased-care systems, and due to the current lack of a Uniform Formulary in the purchased-care system, we designed two separate survey instruments, each specifically tailored to a single system.

Similar domains and questions were used in each survey to provide an overall context and allow for comparison of outcomes from the two survey instruments. For the direct-care prescribers' survey, results are presented by specialty type and by MTF size. For the purchased-care prescribers' survey, results are presented by specialty type and TRICARE patient load. Survey responses are presented by survey topic area. When appropriate, we draw comparisons between responses from the two samples. A detailed set of tables, itemized by survey topic area and survey question, is presented in Appendix D.

Analytic Approach

Before presenting the survey findings, we should mention some standard analytic methods we employed to stratify, weight, and test the results.

Definition of Stratification Variables

To examine potential differences across relevant variables, two stratification variables were created for each survey sample during the sampling process (see Chapter 3 for more details). For the direct-care sample, we examined survey responses by MTF size (defined by the number of providers at the parent installation, with values of *small, medium,* and *large*). MTF size serves as a proxy for the scope of practice at a facility and, hence, for the complexity of the local formulary. Direct-care survey results were also stratified by the type of provider: *primary,* which includes internists, family practitioners, pediatricians, and obstetricians/gynecologists; *secondary,* which includes all specialist physicians; and *physician assistants/advanced practice nurses* (PA/APNs), which include all physician assistants and all advanced nurse practitioners, regardless of practice area.

In the purchased-care sample, we stratified results by provider type and TRICARE patient caseload. As was done with the direct-care sample, prescribers were grouped as either *primary* or *secondary care* providers. Because there were no non-physician prescribers included in the claims database we used for sampling purchased-care providers, we did not create a unique analytic group of PA/APNs.

To examine potential differences by TRICARE caseload, we constructed a two-level variable. This variable was based on the self-reported proportion of TRICARE patients in the prescribers' overall caseload. This approach differs from the sampling strategy in which we used the number of claims submitted to TRICARE in a two-month period to determine differences in caseload (see Chapter 4).

Based on the distribution of self-reported responses (presented later in this chapter), we divided prescribers into two groups: (1) those reporting that TRICARE patients represent fewer than 10 percent or are equal to 10 percent of all their outpatients (classified as a *light* caseload) and (2) those reporting that TRICARE patients represent more than 10 percent of their outpatients (classified as a *heavy* caseload).

Sampling Weights

We used sampling weights to more accurately reflect the population represented in our two sampling frames. Our weighting scheme did not adjust for differences in the likelihood that different types of prescribers responded to the survey. We present both weighted and unweighted distributions of physician characteristics in Table 5.1 to illustrate the effect of the weighting scheme on the composition of the sample. Table 5.1 shows that the weighting scheme does not substantially change the sample distribution of MTF prescribers. The impact of the weighting was more substantial for purchased-care providers, where a relatively small number of high-frequency claimants, pediatricians, and internal medicine sub-specialists were heavily weighted.

In all the following tables in this report, we present unweighted sample sizes within each stratum. However, in those tables that display results by specialty, we weighted by MTF size for the direct-care respondents and by TRICARE patient load for purchased-care respondents. Similarly, we weighted by specialty when presenting results by MTF size and TRICARE patient load.

Table 5.1

Prescriber Characteristics

| | Direct-Care Prescribers | | | Purchased-Care Prescribers | | |
| | | Unweighted | Weighted | | Unweighted | Weighted |
	N	Mean (SD)	Mean (SD)	N	Mean (SD)	Mean (SD)
Age (years)	356	41.0 (8.9)	41.2 (8.0)	205	47.4 (9.2)	49.8 (8.0)
Years in MTF practice						
At current MTF	379	4.7 (4.0)	4.8 (4.1)		Not Applicable	
At other MTFs	382	4.7 (5.8)	4.5 (5.4)		Not Applicable	
Total all MTFs	379	9.4 (7.2)	9.4 (6.9)		Not Applicable	

| | Direct-Care Prescribers | | | | Purchased-Care Prescribers | | | |
| | Unweighted | | Weighted | | Unweighted | | Weighted | |
	N	%	N	%	N	%	N	%
Professional Category								
Physician	323	85	329	86	213	99	206	95
Nurse practitioner	32	8	31	8	3	1	10	5
Physician assistant	26	7	21	6	0	0	0	0
Training Status								
Completed training (e.g., at the attending-physician level)	280	87	277	86	200	96	202	97
In training (resident, intern, or fellow)	27	8	27	9	8	4	6	2
Other	16	5	17	5	1	0	1	1

Table 5.1—Continued

| | Direct-Care Prescribers | | | | Purchased-Care Prescribers | | | |
| | Unweighted | | Weighted | | Unweighted | | Weighted | |
	N	%	N	%	N	%	N	%
Specialty								
Family practice	81	21	77	20	35	17	12	6
General internal med.	35	9	34	9	8	4	4	2
Internal med. subspecialty	61	16	61	16	35	17	25	12
Obstetrics/gynecology	49	13	47	13	21	10	30	14
Pediatrics	85	22	85	22	51	24	85	41
Dermatology	26	7	31	9	22	10	25	11
Other	43	11	44	12	38	18	30	14
Military Status								
Active duty	301	79	297	79	Not Applicable			
Reserve	3	1	5	1	Not Applicable			
Civilian	72	19	73	19	Not Applicable			
Other	1	0	2	1	Not Applicable			
Practice Setting								
Clinic	353	94	354	95	155	72	167	78
Hospital	13	3	12	3	28	13	7	3
Other	8	2	7	1	31	14	40	18
Type of Practice								
Solo practice	Not Assessed				61	28	66	30
Single-specialty group	Not Assessed				111	51	124	57
Multi-specialty group	Not Assessed				31	14	20	9
Other	Not Assessed				13	6	6	3

NOTE: SD = standard deviation.

Statistical Tests

To test for differences in responses across strata, we performed two types of statistical tests. First, we performed simple t-tests of pair-wise differences in means and in proportions across different subgroups within each of the two prescriber groups. Second, we used ordered logit models to test for differences in the distribution of responses across subgroups for survey items for which response categories can be reasonably thought to have an ordinal or Likert scale (Long, 1997, pp. 114–116).

Statistical tests were performed by estimating separate ordered logit models (using the "ologit" command in STATA 7.0) for each of the comparisons of interest (i.e., prescriber specialty and MTF size in the direct-care system and prescriber specialty and TRICARE patient load in the purchased-care system) with indicator variables for the different values of the stratification variables as covariates testing whether the coefficients on the stratification variables were statistically different from zero. The ordered logit approach was used when the dependent variable of interest measured an event frequency or was measured along an ordinal scale (i.e., a measure of agreement or satisfaction).

The advantage of this approach is that it avoids the need to aggregate response categories for the purpose of conducting differences-in-proportions tests in a way that could mask variation across subgroups (i.e., comparing the proportion who agree versus the proportion who are neutral or disagree across subgroups). On the other hand, ordered logit models require more assumptions about the functional form of the process, which gives rise to the observed survey responses (Long, 1997, pp. 140–142).

Prescriber Characteristics

This section presents information on survey respondents' professional characteristics, specialty, practice settings, and workload, and their relationship with TRICARE.

Professional Characteristics

Table 5.1 displays the characteristics of respondents in both survey samples. Within the direct-care sample, the majority of respondents were in their early 40s (mean age 41.2 years, weighted), were on active duty (79 percent), and had been working at their current MTF for just over four and a half years (mean 4.8 years, weighted). In the purchased-care sample, respondents were slightly older, with a mean age of 49.8 years.

Within each sample, the majority of respondents were physicians at the attending level. However, there were four times as many trainee physicians in the direct-care sample as there were in the purchased-care sample (9 percent versus 2 percent, respectively). In both samples, pediatrics was the most commonly reported specialty (22 percent of the direct-care sample and 41 percent of the purchased-care sample, weighted). In the direct-care sample, family practice, internal medicine subspecialties, and obstetrics/gynecology were the next most common specialties. Within the purchased-care sample, pediatrics was followed by obstetrics/gynecology and other specialties (e.g., neurology, nephrology, and other specialties).

Practice Setting and Workload

The majority of respondents in both samples (95 percent of direct-care respondents and 78 percent of purchased-care respondents) reported spending the majority of their outpatient care time in a clinic setting. More than half of the purchased-care respondents (57 percent) indicated that they worked in a single specialty group practice.

Tables 5.2A and 5.2B present the characteristics of prescribers' workloads stratified by MTF size, provider specialty, and patient caseload. Direct-care prescribers reported working an average of 52.1 hours per week. This was roughly comparable with the number of hours (51.9) spent in all professional activities reported by purchased-care prescribers. Purchased-care prescribers reported spending more time in direct patient care than their direct-care counterparts (81.8 percent of their time versus 69.7 percent for direct-care prescribers). Purchased-care prescribers also reported seeing more outpatients per week than direct-care prescribers (108 outpatients versus 69.8 outpatients, respectively). Within the purchased-care sample, primary providers were significantly more likely to see more outpatients per week ($p < 0.01$), and within the direct-care sample, PA/APN providers were significantly more likely to report seeing more outpatients per week ($p < 0.01$). As seen in Tables 5.2A and 5.2B, purchased-care respondents report writing more outpatient prescriptions per week than do direct-care respondents. Within the direct-care sample, PA/APNs tended to write more prescriptions than did primary or secondary prescribers ($p < 0.05$).

Table 5.2.A

Prescriber Workload, Direct-Care Prescribers

	Total (N = 380)	Prescriber by MTF Size			Prescriber by Type of Provider		
		Small (N = 106)	Medium (N = 122)	Large (N = 152)	Primary (N = 209)	Secondary (N = 111)	PA/APN (N = 58)
Average Hours Spent Working at MTF per Week							
Mean	52.1	50.4	52.2	52.5	52.8	55.1	47.2
(SD)	(15.6)	(37.9)	(37.3)	(36.1)	(35.7)	(36.0)	(34.0)
Average Hours per Week in All Professional Activities							
Mean			Not assessed				
(SD)							
Average Number of Outpatients per Week							
Mean	69.8	69.9	67.4	70.5	75.2	49.2	93.6[d, e]
(SD)	(36.7)	(37.9)	(37.3)	(36.1)	(35.7)	(36.0)	(34.0)
Average Time Spent on Patient Care per Week							
Mean	69.7	69.9	67.7	70.3	72.1	58.6	83.3[a, d]
(SD)	(21.84)	(23.5)	(21.8)	(21.3)	(22.0)	(20.7)	(14.2)
Number of Outpatient Medication Prescriptions per Week							
0 to 20 (% of respondents)	11	12	9	11	14	12 [a]	6 [a, c]
21 to 40 (% of respondents)	23	27	26	21	22	27 [a]	17 [a, c]
41 to 60 (% of respondents)	17	17	18	17	13	23 [a]	16 [a, c]
61 to 80 (% of respondents)	16	19	17	15	15	17 [a]	19 [a, c]
81 to 100 (% of respondents)	12	11	15	12	15	9 [a]	10 [a, c]
100 + (% of respondents)	20	15	16	23	20	12 [a]	32 [a, c]

[a]Direct Care: Significant difference from small MTF or from primary care at 0.05 level.

[b]Purchased Care: Significant difference at 0.01 level.

[c]Direct Care: Significant difference from medium-sized MTF or secondary provider at 0.05 level.

[d]Direct Care: Significant difference from medium-sized MTF or secondary provider at 0.01 level.

Table 5.2.B

Prescriber Workload, Purchased-Care Prescribers

	Total (N = 210)	Prescriber by Caseload		Prescriber by Type of Provider	
		Low (N = 130)	High (N = 76)	Primary (N = 112)	Secondary (N = 92)
Average Hours Spent Working at MTF per Week					
Mean			Not applicable		
(SD)					
Average Hours per Week in All Professional Activities					
Mean	51.9	52.4	56.7	55.2	51.6
(SD)	(19.6)	(18.8)	(21.7)	(22.1)	(24.8)
Average Number of Outpatients per Week					
Mean	108	106.3	99.3	123.8 d	93.0
(SD)	(49.1)	(44.4)	(56.0)	(54.1)	(44.9)
Average Time Spent on Patient Care per Week					
Mean	81.8	83.4	82.0	80.9	83.8
(SD)	(14.9)	(12.6)	(15.7)	(15.4)	(13.4)
Number of Outpatient Medication Prescriptions per Week					
0 to 20 (% of respondents)	5	8	11	3	4
21 to 40 (% of respondents)	22	20	24	20	12
41 to 60 (% of respondents)	10	14	9	11	5
61 to 80 (% of respondents)	11	12	14	8	21
81 to 100 (% of respondents)	20	20	14	18	20
100 + (% of respondents)	32	26	28	40	38

Experience and Relationship with TRICARE (Purchased-Care Prescribers Only)

Table 5.3 outlines the purchased-care respondents' relationship and experience with the TRICARE program. As noted, the majority of respondents indicated that they were TRICARE Prime providers. However, one-fifth of respondents did not know or could not recall the nature of their relationship with TRICARE. Providers with a light patient caseload were significantly more likely to report that they did not know the specifics of their contractual relationship. They were also significantly less likely to report being a TRICARE Prime provider (p < 0.01). Primary providers were more likely than secondary providers to report being

Table 5.3

Purchased-Care Prescribers' Relationship with TRICARE

	Total	Prescriber by Caseload		Prescriber by Type of Provider	
		Low	High	Primary	Secondary
Number of Respondents with TRICARE Contractual Arrangement	208	127	78	108	94
Type of TRICARE Contractual Arrangement (% of respondents in category)					
TRICARE Prime provider	64	24[b]	76	69[a]	55
TRICARE Extra provider	1	1	0	0	2
TRICARE Standard provider	16	16	10	15	17
Don't Know	20	59[b]	14	16[a]	26
TRICARE Patients as Percentage of Outpatients					
Number of respondents	186	Not assessed		107	79
Percent of Total Outpatients Who Belong to TRICARE (% of respondents in category)					
Less than 10 percent	37	Not Assessed	Not Assessed	37	34
10 to 24 percent	44	Not Assessed	Not Assessed	43	55
25 to 50 percent	16	Not Assessed	Not Assessed	17	8
Greater than 50 percent	3	Not Assessed	Not Assessed	2	3

Table 5.3—Continued

	Total	Prescriber by Caseload		Prescriber by Type of Provider	
		Low	High	Primary	Secondary
Knowledge about Prescription Dispensing Location					
Number of respondents	212	133	79	113	9
Portion of Patients for Whom Respondents Reported Knowing the Dispensing Location (% of respondents in category)					
None	15	44[a]	12	17	12
Few	12	15[a]	11	14	15
Some	18	13[a]	25	24	17
Most	40	23[a]	38	31	44
All	14	5[a]	14	13	13
Percentage of Respondents Who Are Aware that TRICARE Patients Can Get Free Prescriptions at MTFs	64	48	52	55	45
Percentage of Respondents Who Are Aware that TRICARE Patients Have Different Co-pays Depending on Where Prescription Is Filled	35	43	57	56	44

[a]Purchased Care: Significant difference at 0.05 level.
[b]Purchased Care: Significant difference at 0.01 level.

TRICARE Prime providers and were significantly less likely to report not knowing the specifics of their TRICARE contractual relationship (p < 0.05).

The majority of purchased-care respondents reported that TRICARE patients represented less than 25 percent of their overall patient caseload.

The majority of purchased-care respondents also indicated having at least one year of experience treating TRICARE patients—45 percent indicated that they had been treating TRICARE patients for more than five years, 40 percent had been treating TRICARE patients for more than one year but less than five years, and 1 percent had been treating TRICARE patients for less than one year. Fourteen percent reported that they could not recall how long they had been treating TRICARE patients.

We also asked purchased-care prescribers about their knowledge of the DoD pharmacy benefit and their knowledge of how and where their TRICARE beneficiaries get their prescriptions filled. Forty percent of respondents indicated that they knew where most of their patients filled their prescriptions. Providers with a light TRICARE patient caseload were more likely to report not knowing the dispensing locations for their patients (p < 0.05). On average, 64 percent of purchased-care prescribers knew that TRICARE patients were able to obtain free prescriptions at an MTF, but only 35 percent were aware that TRICARE patients have different co-payments depending on where they get their prescriptions filled.

Prescribers' Familiarity and Experiences with Pharmacy Management Practices

We asked prescribers about their level of familiarity with the content and rules governing formularies, and their level of familiarity with pharmacy management practices more generally. For the direct-care sample, we specifically asked about the formulary at the prescribers' current MTFs. Because there is no TRICARE formulary for network prescribers, we asked prescribers about formularies and preferred-drug lists that applied to *any* patient who had visited their practices in the previous three months. Tables 5.4 and 5.5 summarize their responses to these questions.

Direct-Care Prescribers

Within the direct-care sample (see Table 5.4), all respondents indicated that they were at least somewhat familiar with the drugs contained in their MTF

Table 5.4

Direct-Care Prescribers' Familiarity with Formularies

	Total (N = 382)	Prescriber by MTF Size			Prescriber by Type of Provider		
		Small (N = 108)	Medium (N = 122)	Large (N = 151)	Primary (N = 211)	Secondary (N = 112)	PA/APN (N = 59)
		Percentage of Respondents					
Familiarity with Drugs in Formularies							
Very familiar	63	59	70	62	59	70	67
Somewhat familiar	37	42	30	38	40	29	32
Not at all familiar	0	0	0	0	1	1	0
Familiarity with Rules and Procedures for Prescribing Non-Formulary Drugs							
Very familiar	60	38	67[b, d]	65[b, d]	55	66	53
Somewhat familiar	37	59	30[b, d]	31[b, d]	41	32	41
Not at all familiar	4	3	2[b, d]	4[b, d]	4	2	6
Source of Knowledge About Content of Formularies (respondents checked any that applied)							
Examine formulary list	32	37	33[a]	30	35	30	41
Notice from electronic prescribing menu	69	63	78	67	68	74	60
Feedback from pharmacy	25	17	27[a]	27	24	23	29
Patients inform prescriber	8	5	10	9	7	5	18[a, c]
Prescriber relies on my memory	43	38	39	47	42	40	55

[a]Direct Care: Significant difference from small MTF or from primary care at 0.05 level.

[b]Direct Care: Significant differences from small MTF or from primary care at 0.01 level.

[c]Direct Care: Significant difference from medium-sized MTF or secondary provider at 0.05 level.

[d]Test of equivalence of distribution of responses.

Table 5.5

Purchased-Care Prescribers' Familiarity and Experience with Formularies and Preferred-Drug Lists

	Total	Prescriber by Caseload		Prescriber by Type of Provider	
		Light	Heavy	Primary	Secondary
Number of Respondents Who Prescribe Medications Based on Formularies or Preferred-Drug Lists	192	116	79	102	85
Respondents Who Have Prescribed Medications Based on Formularies or Preferred-Drug Lists in Past Three Months (% of respondents)[c]	92	79[a]	91	95	90
Number of Formulary Lists Used by Prescribers[c]					
Number of respondents	159	91	65	89	66
None (% of respondents in category)	0	0	1	3[b,d]	0
1–2 lists (% of respondents in category)	23	18	14	11[b,d]	22
3–5 lists (% of respondents in category)	37	37	29	31[b,d]	29
More than 5 lists (% of respondents in category)	40	38	18	43[b,d]	17
Level of Familiarity with Drugs in Formularies					
Number of respondents	155	91	61	85	66
Very familiar (% of respondents in category)	23	20	26	27[a,d]	13
Somewhat familiar (% of respondents in category)	64	63	62	52[a,d]	75
Not at all familiar (% of respondents in category)	12	17	12	9[a,d]	12
Familiarity with Rules and Procedures for Prescribing Non-Formulary Drugs					
Number of respondents	155	90	60	84	65
Very familiar (% of respondents in category)	10	4	9	12[a,d]	12
Somewhat familiar (% of respondents in category)	70	65	71	73[a,d]	55
Not at all familiar (% of respondents in category)	20	30	20	15[a,d]	35

Table 5.5—Continued

	Total	Prescriber by Caseload		Prescriber by Type of Provider	
		Light	Heavy	Primary	Secondary
Percentage of Outpatients Covered by Formularies[c]					
Number of respondents	149	85	61	84	61
Less than 10 percent (% of respondents in category)	3	6[a,d]	2	3[b,d]	5
10–24 percent (% of respondents in category)	21	33[a,d]	17	7[b,d]	35
25–50 percent (% of respondents in category)	42	31[a,d]	48	45[b,d]	25
More than 50 percent (% of respondents in category)	34	29[a,d]	33	44[b,d]	35
Number of Preferred Drug Lists Used by Prescribers[c]					
Number of Respondents	158	90	65	88	66
None (% of respondents in category)	7	9[a,d]	8	5[a,d]	10
1–2 lists (% of respondents in category)	27	33[a,d]	25	19[a,d]	35
3–5 lists (% of respondents in category)	42	30[a,d]	50	52[a,d]	31
More than 5 lists (% of respondents in category)	24	27[a,d]	16	25[a,d]	23
Level of Familiarity with Drugs on Preferred Drug Lists					
Number of respondents	147	83	61	82	61
Very familiar (% of respondents in category)	15	17	13	16	20
Somewhat familiar (% of respondents in category)	64	59	75	67	64
Not at all familiar (% of respondents in category)	21	24	13	16	15
Level of Familiarity with Rules and Procedures for Prescribing Non-Preferred Drugs					
Number of Respondents	147	83	61	82	61
Very familiar (% of respondents in category)	9	5	8	12	10
Somewhat familiar (% of respondents in category)	66	70	70	68	64
Not at all familiar (% of respondents in category)	24	25	22	21	25

Table 5.5—Continued

	Total	Prescriber by Caseload		Prescriber by Type of Provider	
		Light	Heavy	Primary	Secondary
Percentage of Patients Covered by Preferred-Drug Lists[c]					
Number of Respondents	139	76	60	78	57
Less than 10 percent (% of respondents in category)	8	13[a,d]	3	6[a,d]	16
10–24 percent (% of respondents in category)	34	38[a,d]	37	27[a,d]	36
25–50 percent (% of respondents in category)	33	32[a,d]	34	38[a,d]	29
More than 50 percent (% of respondents in category)	24	17[a,d]	26	29[a,d]	18
How Prescriber Determines Which Drugs Are in the Formulary or on the Preferred-Drug List Under Patient's Health Plan					
Number of respondents					
"Look at written formulary/list" (% of respondents in category)	14	13	16	16	11
"Know by memory" (% of respondents in category)	9	5	14	8	8
"Write what I think is on form/list and assume pharmacist will call if it is not on the list" (% of respondents in category)	60	60	59	64	54
"Ask staff to find out if drug is covered" (% of respondents in category)	5	6	5	5	6
"It is patient's responsibility to find out and inform me" (% of respondents in category)	7	9	5	6	9
Other method of determination (% of respondents in category)	6	8	2	1	12

[a]Purchased Care: Significant difference at 0.05 level.
[b]Purchased Care: Significant difference at 0.01 level.
[c]Excludes "don't know" responses.
[d]Test of equivalence of distribution of responses.

formulary. No statistically significant differences were observed by MTF size or by provider specialty. The majority of MTF respondents were at least somewhat familiar with the rules and procedures for prescribing non-formulary medications. Providers in small facilities were less likely to report being "very familiar" with the rules and procedures than were providers in medium or large facilities ($p < 0.01$).

When asked about the source of their knowledge of the content of the formulary, the majority of respondents indicated using more than one source. A notice from an electronic prescribing menu, such as might be generated by the CHCS, was the most commonly endorsed mechanism for finding out if an item is on the formulary. While few prescribers overall reported relying on patients to tell them whether certain items are on the formulary, PA/APN prescribers were more likely than physicians to rely on the patient for this information ($p < 0.05$).

Purchased-Care Prescribers

Because no formulary exists for TRICARE beneficiaries, we asked purchased-care prescribers about their general experience and familiarity with any specific formularies and/or preferred-drug lists.

The vast majority of purchased-care prescribers had recent experience with formularies or preferred-drug lists, with 92 percent of respondents reporting that they prescribed medications based on formularies or preferred-drug lists in the previous three months. Most purchased-care respondents (76 percent) indicated that more than a quarter of their patients had pharmacy benefits governed by a formulary. Fewer respondents (57 percent) indicated that more than a quarter of their patients' pharmacy benefits was governed by preferred-drug lists.

These responses varied significantly by patient caseload and by type of provider. For example, primary providers were more likely than secondary providers to report having a higher percentage of patients with pharmacy benefits restricted by formularies or preferred drug lists ($p < 0.01$). This finding may reflect the fact that primary-care providers care for a wide variety of conditions and patient populations and thus may encounter restrictions more often.

Of those prescribers having experience with formularies and preferred-drug lists in the previous three months, 77 percent reported using more than three formulary lists and 66 percent reported using more than three preferred-drug lists. These findings varied somewhat by type of provider, with primary providers more likely than secondary providers to report having been exposed to more than five formularies (43 percent of primary providers versus 17 percent of secondary providers [p<0.01]) and exposed to more than three preferred-drug lists during those three months (77 percent of primary providers versus 54 percent of secondary providers [p < 0.05]).

Nearly 87 percent of purchased-care providers indicated being at least somewhat familiar with the content of formularies, and 80 percent reported being at least somewhat familiar with the rules and procedures for prescribing non-formulary medications. Primary providers were more likely than secondary providers to report being very familiar with the rules and procedures for prescribing non-formulary medications and were more likely than secondary providers to report being at least somewhat familiar with them (p < 0.05).

With regard to the preferred-drug lists, 79 percent of purchased-care prescribers were at least somewhat familiar with their content, and 75 percent of purchased-care prescribers reported being at least somewhat familiar with the rules and procedures for prescribing non-preferred drugs. The findings on familiarity with formularies varied by provider type (p < 0.05), but the findings on familiarity with preferred-drug lists did not vary by provider type.

It is unclear why these differences were found between the level of familiarity with preferred-drug lists and the level of familiarity with formularies, but one possibility is that formularies have more clearly defined boundaries as to when a patient can or cannot obtain a drug without approval. More specifically, in the case of formulary management, pharmacists often inform clinicians that a drug is not generally available under the insurance plan. With preferred lists, the drug is available, but it is up to the patient to inform the clinician that he or she has a higher co-payment for that drug.

When asked about their source of knowledge regarding the content of formularies or preferred-drug lists, the majority of respondents (60 percent) indicated that they typically write a prescription for what they think is on the formulary or preferred-drug list and assume that the pharmacist will call them if it isn't. Very few (9 percent) report knowing the content of the formulary or list by memory, and only 14 percent report actually examining a written list before writing a prescription.

Acknowledging that the two types of survey respondents—direct-care and purchased-care—were responding on the basis of two different systems and that the questions were framed slightly differently in the two surveys, we nevertheless found that the likelihood of direct-care prescribers reporting being familiar with the content and rules of the MTF formulary was far greater than the likelihood of network prescribers reporting being familiar with their respective formularies (see Figure 5.1). There is also a difference in the prescribers' source of

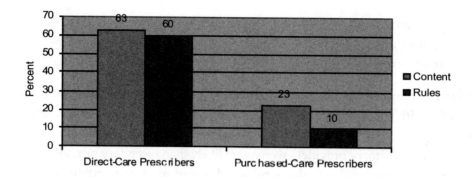

Figure 5.1—Percentage of Direct-Care Prescribers Versus Purchased-Care Prescribers Who Are Very Familiar with Formulary Content and Rules

knowledge on what is or is not included on the formulary (for example, only 25 percent of direct-care providers wait for feedback from the pharmacy).

One explanation for such differences is that purchased-care prescribers reported interacting with many more formularies in the previous three months than did direct-care providers. The majority of purchased-care prescribers reported interacting with more than five formularies or preferred-drug lists, and only one-fifth reported dealing with just one or two lists during that time. Therefore, it might be expected that purchased-care prescribers would be less familiar than direct-care prescribers with the actual content and rules for all the formularies and lists they must follow.

Impact of Pharmacy Management Practices on Prescribers' Clinical Practice

To better understand prescribers' perceptions of the impact that formularies have on their clinical practice, we asked how frequently their prescribing behavior had been altered due to formulary restrictions. More specifically, we asked prescribers to indicate how often in the past three months they (1) changed a medication prescription because the medication was not available on the formulary; (2) chose not to prescribe a non-formulary drug because they thought the request would be denied; (3) chose not to prescribe a non-formulary drug because they thought the request/approval process would take too long; (4) were asked by a patient to prescribe a non-formulary drug even though the prescriber believed the formulary drug was just as effective; or (5) advised the patient to obtain a non-formulary drug outside the MTF (for direct-care respondents only). Figure 5.2 illustrates the percentage of respondents who reported that their

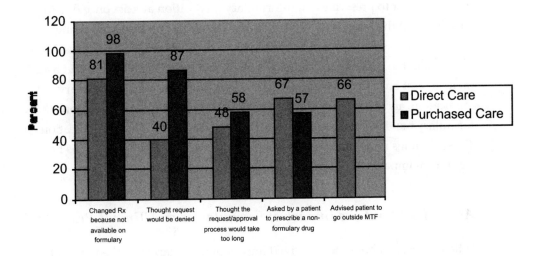

Figure 5.2—Percentage of Respondents Whose Prescribing Behavior Changed over the Past Three Months Due to Formulary Restrictions

prescribing behavior had been altered in any of these ways. More detailed data, stratified by subgroups of respondents, can be found in Appendix D.

Within the direct-care system, 80 percent of respondents indicated that at least once during the previous three months they had changed a medication they had originally prescribed because the drug was not in the formulary. When asked if the request process discouraged them from prescribing non-formulary medications, 40 percent reported that they chose not to prescribe a non-formulary medication due to a concern that the request would be denied, and 48 percent reported that at least once in the previous three months they chose not to prescribe a non-formulary medication because the request/approval process would take too long.

Sixty-six percent of direct-care respondents reported that at least once during the previous three months they advised patients to obtain a non-formulary drug outside the MTF, and 67 percent reported that at least once in the past three months a patient asked them to prescribe a non-formulary medication even though the prescriber believed the formulary medication was just as effective. A substantially greater number of purchased-care prescribers than direct-care prescribers reported changing their original medication choice for another medication at least once in the past three months because the medication was not on a formulary.

The perception that prescriptions for non-formulary medications will be denied is much greater among purchased-care prescribers than it is among direct-care prescribers. Eighty-seven percent of purchased-care prescribers reported that they chose not to prescribe a non-formulary medication at least once due to concerns that the request would be denied; 58 percent reported not doing so at least once due to a belief that the request would take too long to process. More than half of the purchased-care respondents indicated that a patient had asked them at least once in the prior three months to prescribe a non-formulary medication, and 57 percent reported actually making a request for a non-formulary medication because the patient requested a particular medication. These findings may indicate that patient preference for medications has had a significant impact on prescribing behavior.

Attitudes About the Impact of Formularies on Clinical Practice

When we asked about the perceived impact of formularies on their clinical practice and decisionmaking abilities, we found that direct-care prescribers were substantially more likely to report that formularies helped them to prescribe clinically appropriate medications than were purchased-care prescribers (64 percent versus 9 percent, respectively). However, there were no significant variations among prescriber subgroups (e.g., primary versus secondary providers).

Twice as many direct-care prescribers as purchased-care prescribers reported that they believed their patients could get non-formulary medications when it is medically justified (93 percent versus 45 percent, respectively). Direct-care prescribers in large MTFs were significantly more likely than those in small and medium-sized MTFs to agree that patients could get non-formulary medications when medically justified ($p < 0.01$), and PA/APN prescribers were significantly less likely than other types of providers to agree with this statement ($p < 0.05$).

Improving Compliance with Pharmacy Benefits

We also asked prescribers to choose from among a number of items that might make it easier for them to comply with formulary lists (see Table D.3 in Appendix D). Within both the direct-care and purchased-care settings, the item "regularly updated lists" was selected by more than half of the respondents. "Regular reminders on content" was the item endorsed most frequently by purchased-care respondents (62 percent indicated it would help them comply with formulary lists). Direct-care respondents tended to select "electronic prescribing" more frequently than did purchased-care respondents. Far fewer purchased-care respondents than direct-care respondents thought that feedback on prescription patterns would be helpful (12 percent versus 42 percent, respectively). We suspect that this difference may be because private clinicians must deal with multiple lists and formularies, and therefore the feedback would generate multiple assessments and consequently much more time-consuming work, unlike the situation with prescribers in the MTFs who have only one formulary to contend with. Within the direct-care sample, PA/APN prescribers were more likely to select "regular reminders on content" and less likely to select "electronic prescribing" than their primary or secondary provider counterparts ($p < 0.01$).

Attitudes on Effectiveness and Goals of Pharmacy Management Practices

The findings we report in this section and the next one reflect substantially more confidence in the effectiveness and goals of pharmacy management practices among direct-care providers than among purchased-care providers (see Table 5.6). Across every question, more than twice as many direct-care respondents as purchased-care respondents were in agreement with statements about the effectiveness and goals of pharmacy management practices. Apart from having less-positive attitudes about tracking changes in formularies (see Table D.4 in Appendix D), the attitudes of direct-care providers toward pharmacy management practices were substantially more positive than those of their purchased-care counterparts.

We found significant differences of opinion in this area among subgroups of providers within the direct-care system. Secondary providers were less likely to agree than primary providers that formularies have done a good job of keeping up to date the list of drugs available within the drug classes that they would like to prescribe ($p < 0.05$). PA/APN prescribers were less likely to agree than other types of providers that it is important for MTFs to save money by choosing the best drug with the best value within its therapeutic class ($p < 0.05$). PA/APN prescribers were also less likely than other types of providers to agree that they were satisfied with the non-formulary waiver/approval processes at their MTF ($p < 0.05$).

No significant differences were observed among subgroups of respondents in the purchased-care sample.

Opinions on the Role and Effectiveness of P&T Committees

We asked a series of questions about prescribers' perceptions of P&T committees. For the direct-care sample, questions were aimed at their opinions about the P&T

Table 5.6

Prescribers in Agreement with Statements About Pharmacy Management Practices

	Direct-Care Prescribers (%) (N = 382)	Purchased-Care Prescribers (%) (N = 162)
It is easy to keep track of changes to formularies/lists	47	10
Formularies/lists have done a good job keeping drugs up-to-date in the classes I would like to prescribe	67	15
It is important for health plans/MTFs to save money by choosing for the lists the best drug with the best value within its therapeutic class	87	40
The drug restrictions imposed by formularies/lists are necessary for containing costs in a health plan/MTF	80	33
Overall, I am satisfied with the non-formulary waiver approval process in my MTF	78	N/A

committee at their own MTF, whereas for the purchased-care sample, questions were aimed at opinions about P&T committees in general.

Within the direct-care system, 79 percent of respondents indicated they were at least somewhat familiar with the activities of the P&T committee at their MTF. Prescribers in medium-sized facilities were less likely to report being familiar with the P&T committee. Overall, direct-care prescribers reported being satisfied with the decisions and actions of their P&T committee (with no statistical variation among subgroups of respondents).

We asked both samples their opinions about the actions of P&T committees. The vast majority of direct-care prescribers agreed that their P&T committee was responsive to their concerns, believed the committee would choose the safest and most clinically effective drugs, and choose drugs with the best value in their class. Far fewer network prescribers agreed to the same statements. (Table D.5 in Appendix D provides a breakdown of these responses stratified by subgroup.) These differences of opinion between direct-care and purchased-care prescribers mirror the differences in attitudes about formulary management practices in general (shown in Table 5.7).

Table 5.7

Prescribers in Agreement with Statements About P&T Committees

	Direct-Care Prescribers (%) (N = 305)	Purchased-Care Prescribers (%) (N = 162)
P&T committees are responsive to the concerns of providers	84	34
I have confidence in the ability of P&T committees to choose the safest and most clinically effective drugs	83	23
I have confidence in the ability of P&T committees to choose the drugs with the best value	88	20

Impact of Non-Formulary Prescriptions Written Outside of MTFs (Direct-Care Prescribers Only)

Military beneficiaries are able to obtain prescriptions at MTFs at no cost, regardless of who writes the prescription, provided the drug is on the MTF formulary. If a drug is not available because it is not on the formulary, and the patient desires to obtain a non-formulary medication (for the same medical condition for which the formulary medication was prescribed), a new prescription is needed (written by either a direct-care or non-direct-care prescriber). If the patient still desires the non-formulary medication to be filled by the MTF at no cost, a direct-care prescriber must make a special purchase request. Rewriting prescriptions that are originally written outside an MTF so that they may be filled at the MTF is discouraged by MTF commanders.

To learn more about the frequency and impact of such requests, we asked direct-care prescribers a series of questions about the number of times they have rewritten prescriptions and their perceived impact of outside prescriptions on the workload and resources of the MTF. As seen in Figure 5.3, more than half of the direct-care prescribers in all subgroups agreed that rewriting prescriptions for non-formulary medications (originally written by non-MTF prescribers) was burdensome to prescribers. Less than half of the direct-care prescribers agree that filling prescriptions that are written outside the MTF drains MTF resources. Prescribers in medium-sized MTFs were more likely to agree that patients filling prescriptions written by outside providers drains MTF resources and that rewriting prescriptions is burdensome to prescribers at the MTF ($p < 0.01$).

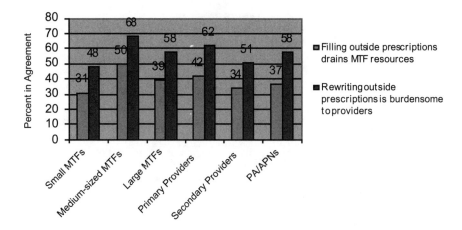

Figure 5.3—Opinions on Impact of Prescriptions Written by Non-MTF Providers, by MTF Size and Provider Category, Direct-Care Prescribers Only

We also asked direct-care prescribers how often they had rewritten prescriptions and requested a non-formulary medication at the patient's request. In general, direct-care prescribers did not report rewriting prescriptions (from a non-MTF prescriber) very often. (See Table D.6 in Appendix D.) Only 13 percent reported doing so more than five times in the previous three months. Prescribers in large facilities were more likely than those in small or medium-sized facilities to rewrite prescriptions more frequently (i.e., more than five times over the previous three months).

Direct-care prescribers also reported that they rarely requested non-formulary medications (originally prescribed outside the MTF) just because the patient wanted to fill the prescription at the MTF (63 percent reported never having done so in the previous three months). Prescribers in large MTFs were more likely to report never requesting non-formulary medications at the patient's request (p < 0.05). We further asked direct-care prescribers what their initial action would be for a hypothetical patient who was taking a non-formulary medication. Overwhelmingly (86 percent of respondents), direct-care prescribers reported that they would convert the patient to a similar drug that was on the formulary.

Prescribers' Experiences with Obtaining Approval for Non-Formulary and Non-Preferred Drugs

Prescribers were asked a series of questions about their opinions of and experiences with obtaining approval for non-formulary or non-preferred medications. Specifically, we asked how often they made such requests and what happened after the most recent request. If the request was denied, we asked what impact, if any, the denial had on the patient's health and what actions the prescriber subsequently took (e.g., appealed the decision or prescribed another medication).

Experiences with Making Requests for Non-Formulary Medications

To better understand prescribers' perceived access to non-formulary medications and to solicit their opinions about the non-formulary approval process, we asked a series of questions about their experiences with making non-formulary medication requests.

As seen in Table 5.8, a large majority of prescribers in both samples indicated that they had recent experiences with requesting non-formulary medications. Within the direct-care system, the majority of respondents indicated that their requests were approved relatively quickly (53 percent said the requests were approved in two days or less). Prescribers in the purchased-care sample reported having far fewer non-formulary requests approved than their counterparts in the direct-care sample (73 percent versus 96 percent, respectively). The higher rate of non-formulary request approvals in the direct-care system may help explain why the threat of being denied the request for a non-formulary medication has little impact on direct-care providers.

It is important to note here that the survey respondents were reporting about two very different systems. Direct-care prescribers were responding about their experiences within their own MTFs, whereas purchased-care prescribers were responding about their overall experiences with formularies and preferred-drug lists. As we noted earlier in this chapter, purchased-care prescribers deal with multiple systems and, as such, we cannot directly compare the current non-formulary request/waiver process between the two systems.

Actions After Most-Recent Request Denial

We also asked prescribers who had made a non-formulary request in the previous three months, and who had reported that one or more of these requests had been denied, about the actions they had taken after the most-recent denial for a non-formulary medication. Table 5.9 summarizes the responses from direct- and purchased-care prescribers.

Table 5.8

Prescribers' Experience with Requests for Non-Formulary Medications

	Direct-Care Prescribers		Purchased-Care Prescribers	
	N	%	N	%
Have you ever requested approval for a non-formulary or non-preferred drug?	379	88	160	84
Mean percentage of requests made in previous three months that were approved	314	96	99	73
Percentage of requests approved in two days or less	292	53	N/A	N/A
Percentage of requests approved in more than five days	292	27	N/A	N/A
	N	Mean	N	Mean
Number of non-formulary requests in the previous three months	314	7.2	114	10.4

Denials within the direct-care system were reported less than 5 percent of the time, and in the most recent instance of a denial, only 13 percent of direct-care prescribers noted resubmitting the request, and 20 percent indicated that they advised the patient to obtain the medication outside the MTF (see Table 5.9).

Within the purchased-care system, in which denials were perceived to occur a bit more often than within the direct-care system, 45 percent of prescribers reported prescribing a formulary medication upon denial of the non-formulary request. Forty-four percent of purchased-care respondents indicated that they resubmitted the request with additional information, and 25 percent reported that they appealed the denial. (Table D.7 in Appendix D provides a detailed breakdown of these results stratified by provider subgroups.)

Impact of Non-Formulary Request Denials on Patients' Health

For prescribers who reported a recent denial for a non-formulary medication, we asked about the impact that the most recent denial had on the patient's health. Figure 5.4 shows the responses from direct- and purchased-care prescribers. The majority of respondents in both samples indicated that the denial did not impact the patient's health or that it was too soon to determine if the denial had an impact. However, a greater number of purchased-care prescribers reported some decline (either major or minor) in the patient's health as a result of the denial. Within the direct-care sample, prescribers in medium-sized MTFs (51 percent) were more likely than those in small MTFs (5 percent) or large MTFs (22 percent) to report that it was too soon to determine if the denial had any impact on the patient's health. Non-physician prescribers were more likely than primary or

Table 5.9

Prescribers' Actions Taken After Most-Recent Denial of a Request for Non-Formulary Medication

	Direct-Care Respondents (%) (N = 146)	Purchased-Care Respondents (%) (N = 85)
Appealed	8	25
Resubmitted request	13	44
Sought approval for a different non-formulary drug	1	13
Prescribed a formulary drug	9	45
Advised patient to obtain drug outside the MTF	20	n/a
Other	5	13

NOTE: Respondents checked all answers that applied.

secondary prescribers to report that the patient's health was unaffected (71 percent of PA/APNs versus 53 percent of primary and secondary providers).

Within the purchased-care sample, primary providers were more likely than secondary providers to report that the patient's health was unaffected (62 percent versus 16 percent, respectively [p < 0.01]), and secondary providers were more likely than primary providers to report a decline in the patient's health (67 versus 10 percent, respectively [p < 0.01]). (Table D.7 in Appendix D contains the frequency of responses stratified by prescriber subgroups.)

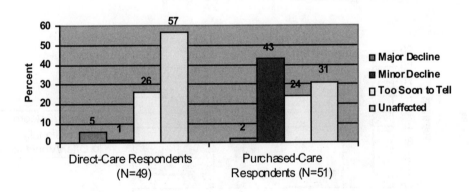

Figure 5.4—Perceived Effect of Most Recent Denial on Patient's Health

Effects of Pharmacy Management and Direct-to-Consumer Marketing on Patient Behavior

To better understand the ways in which pharmacy management and DTC advertising affect patient behavior, we asked prescribers about the number of complaints they received from patients, their perceptions of the effects of tiered co-payment systems, and their perceptions of the impact of DTC advertising on their patients' demand for pharmaceuticals.

Patients' Complaints About Drug Costs and Availability

We asked providers in both survey groups about the frequency of complaints they received from patients about out-of-pocket expenses for prescriptions. Figure 5.5 compares the responses of direct-care and purchased-care providers. In both systems, the majority of providers said that their patients never or seldom complained about out-of-pocket expenses.

Within the direct-care sample, PA/APNs reported receiving complaints from patients about out-of-pocket expenses for prescriptions significantly more often than did secondary providers ($p < 0.05$). This result may be due to a number of factors including PA/APNs writing a higher overall volume of prescriptions, or because patients feel more comfortable expressing their disapproval to non-physicians. No significant variations by provider subgroup were observed in the purchased-care sample. (See Table D.8 in Appendix D).

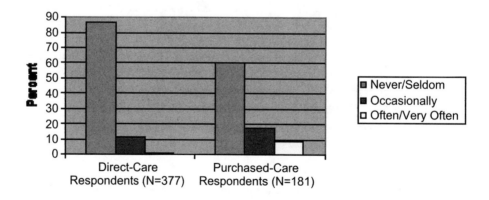

Figure 5.5—Frequency of Patient Complaints About Out-of-Pocket Expenses

Effects of Tiered Co-Payment Systems (Purchased-Care Prescribers Only)

Purchased-care prescribers were queried about their perceptions of the effectiveness of tiered co-payments for pharmaceuticals and their effect on patients. Table 5.10 shows little percentage variation by caseload and provider type in response to statements about tiered co-payment systems. Less than half of the purchased-care prescribers agreed that tiered co-payment systems promote cost-effective prescribing. However, more prescribers with light caseloads than with heavy caseloads and more secondary than primary providers agreed with this statement (54 percent versus 40 percent, and 56 percent versus 44 percent, respectively). Opinions are split, however, on whether a tiered co-payment system places an unfair burden on patients. Thirty-six percent of purchased-care providers agreed with the statement, the same percentage was neutral, and 28 percent disagreed with it (see Table D.9 in Appendix D). When asked if a tiered co-payment system limits the effect of drug advertising, about half of the respondents were neutral on the subject (48 percent).

Perceived Impact of Direct-to-Consumer Marketing

When we asked prescribers about the frequency of patient requests for advertised drugs in the past three months, a majority of providers in both samples (90 percent of purchased-care prescribers and 77 percent of direct-care

Table 5.10

Purchased-Care Prescribers' Responses to Statements About the Effectiveness of Tiered Co-Payment Systems and Their Effect on Patients

	Total (N = 214)	Caseload		Provider Type	
		Light (N = 131)	Heavy (N = 78)	Primary (N = 114)	Secondary (N = 95)
A tiered co-payment system promotes cost-effective prescribing	44	54	40	44	56
A tiered co-payment system places an unfair burden on patients	36	37	34	36	44
A tiered co-payment system limits the effect of drug advertising	33	38	26	34	33

prescribers) indicated that they received such a request at least once. Roughly a third (33 percent of purchased-care prescribers and 38 percent of direct-care prescribers) reported more than five such requests in the previous three months.

Within the direct-care system, a higher percentage of PA/APNs reported getting more than 20 requests from patients for advertised drugs than did primary or secondary providers (p < 0.01) (see Figure 5.6). Within the purchased-care system, providers with a light caseload were more likely than those with a heavy caseload to say that in the previous three months they had not received a request for a drug because a patient had seen it advertised (p < 0.05). In addition, when asked specifically about requests from TRICARE patients, 53 percent of purchased-care providers reported that TRICARE patients seldom asked for drugs they have seen advertised, and 31 percent reported that TRICARE patients made such requests at least occasionally.

We asked providers in both samples a series of questions to assess their perceptions of DTC advertising. Overall, almost half of the prescribers in both samples (48 percent for the direct-care sample and 47 percent for purchased-care sample) said DTC advertising prompted patients to seek health care for conditions that might otherwise go untreated. Roughly half of the prescribers in both groups also reported that patients' requests for advertised drugs made their jobs more challenging (56 percent of direct-care prescribers versus 46 percent of purchased-care prescribers).

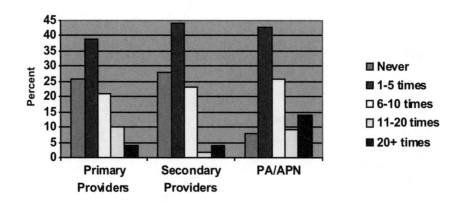

Figure 5.6—Number of Times Patients Request a Drug Because It Was Seen Advertised, by Type of Provider, Direct-Care Prescribers Only

Perceptions of TRICARE Patients' Access to Pharmaceuticals (Purchased-Care Prescribers Only)

To learn more about TRICARE patients' concerns about their access to pharmaceuticals in general, we asked purchased-care prescribers how often their TRICARE patients complained about the lack of availability of a drug (see Figure 5.7).

Seventy-seven percent of purchased-care providers reported that patients complained at least occasionally about drugs not being available at an MTF pharmacy. Fewer purchased-care prescribers reported hearing complaints at least occasionally about non-availability of drugs through the NMOP.

We also asked purchased-care providers how often they advise TRICARE patients to fill prescriptions at the MTF. Almost half (48 percent) indicated they did so often or very often. Earlier in this chapter, we reported that 64 percent of purchased-care providers were aware that TRICARE patients could obtain free prescriptions at an MTF. Providers with light caseloads were significantly more likely than those with heavy caseloads to *never* advise patients to go to their MTF (57 percent versus 26 percent, respectively [p < 0.05]). Primary providers were more likely than secondary providers to say that they never advise TRICARE patients to get their prescriptions filled at their MTF. (See Table D.11 in Appendix D for details.)

Respondents' Write-In Comments

Direct-care and purchased-care providers were given the opportunity to write in comments with respect to their overall opinions and thoughts on the survey

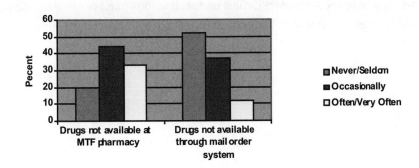

Figure 5.7—Frequency of Complaints Heard About Access to Pharmaceuticals, Purchased-Care Prescribers Only

topics. (The comments from both samples can be found in Appendix E.) Both groups of prescribers offered ample commentary on a range of issues addressed within the survey and on issues with regard to the MHS overall, the field of medicine, and managed care.

We categorized the general comments we received from purchased-care providers as follows: pharmacy issues, insurance or formulary burden, quality of life, cost, formulary content, quality of care, the TRICARE program (coverage/reimbursement policies), communication, and miscellaneous. In general, purchased-care prescribers expressed dissatisfaction and frustration with formulary management (e.g., having to keep current with multiple drug lists and other complaints) and with TRICARE (e.g., complaints about speed of reimbursement and TRICARE management).

General comments from direct-care prescribers were categorized as follows: pharmacy staff, formulary content, cost, quality of life, outside prescriptions/pharmacies, quality of care, non-formulary approval processes, and other/miscellaneous. Direct-care respondents expressed some frustration with the current system and processes (e.g., the burden on the MTF budget, the workload burden from non-MTF prescriptions, the difficulty in keeping up with formulary changes, the lack of uniformity across the MHS), but they also had several commendations for the pharmacy staff and recommendations for greater flexibility of the formulary system within their own MTF.

Direct-care prescribers were given the opportunity to write in specific responses to the question, If you had the opportunity, what changes would you make to the content, policies, and/or procedures of your MTF's formulary? Those comments were categorized as follows: no problems; cost; non-formulary issues (e.g., products and procedures); formulary content (e.g., suggestions on additions); patient issues (e.g., making policies clearer to patients); process (e.g., paperwork demands due to the formulary); rules and restrictions (e.g., restricting access to non-MTF prescriptions at MTFs); communication; and miscellaneous.

6. Conclusions

This chapter provides a synopsis of the findings of the baseline survey of prescribers conducted within both the direct-care (i.e., MTF) and purchased-care (i.e., network) systems. We first review the limitations of the study, then discuss the findings for each sample separately, and finally, where possible, we compare findings across the two systems.

Study Limitations

Some limitations of this study should be noted:

First, because we did not have data describing the universe of prescribers within the MHS, the survey data noted in this report represent the feedback of only the sample population and cannot be generalized to all MHS prescribers.

In addition, given the low response rate within the purchased-care sample, there is the risk of non-response bias within the results from this particular sample. On the one hand, if purchased-care prescribers who dislike formulary management in general did not participate in this study, the results would probably underestimate the negative attitudes and perceptions reported by purchased-care respondents. On the other hand, if purchased-care prescribers who generally favor formulary management did not participate, then the negative attitudes reported within this sample are probably overestimated.

Another limitation of the study includes the lack of documented information about any special administrative procedures within the direct-care system for non-physician prescribers. Anecdotal reports from MTF physicians indicate that non-physician prescribers are faced with a much different subset of administrative requirements for managing their prescribing behavior than are physicians, and non-physician prescribers may also be targeted differently than physicians by pharmaceutical industry marketing (i.e., physician detailing).

Because our study did not include a special survey instrument for non-physician prescribers, we did not particularly capture any of the potential effects on non-physicians' prescribing behaviors or attitudes stemming from any special administrative requirements. As such, the responses from non-physician prescribers must be interpreted with care. Although they were included in our population for both samples (and were mandated for inclusion by the NDAA for

76

FY 2000, Public Law 106-65), non-physician prescribers were not well represented within the purchased-care sample due to their low number of submitted claims during our sampling time frame (September 1 through November 30, 2000).

Finally, it should be noted that the baseline survey did not assess MHS prescribers' attitudes about and experiences with prescribing medications that require prior authorization. While prior authorization is a tool in formulary management, and there is research literature to demonstrate its impact on utilization and costs (Smalley et al., 1995), given the lack of a current UF management system across the MHS and the differing implementation policies for prior authorizations within dispensing locations in the direct-care system, we did not specifically assess experiences with prior authorizations. We expect that after the UF is implemented, our basis for comparing prescribers' attitudes and experiences with prior authorizations will be more sound; thus, the follow-up survey instrument will include questions that address prior authorizations.

Findings Regarding Direct-Care System Prescribers

The majority of direct-care prescribers reported being very familiar with the formulary and formulary management systems in their MTFs. They reported favorable opinions about P&T committees and seemed to understand and endorse the need for pharmacy management techniques in controlling costs. They also strongly believed that formularies are a valuable tool in their clinical decisionmaking. They reported having experiences requesting non-formulary medications and believed that patients can get access to non-formulary medications when the need is justified. Direct-care prescribers also reported that denials of non-formulary requests are rare, and over half of them reported that such denials do not negatively impact their patients' health status.

More than half of the direct-care prescribers reported that it is difficult to keep track of changes to formularies, but the majority believed that formularies are up to date for the classes of drugs they wish to prescribe. They indicated that regular updates and electronic prescribing or electronic reminders would improve and ease compliance with formularies.

In general, direct-care system prescribers indicated a high level of familiarity and comfort with the current MHS formularies and formulary management practices in general.

While some differences were noted within the sample of direct-care prescribers— for example between physician and non-physician prescribers and among prescribers in small, medium-sized, and large facilities—without additional multivariate analyses, it is premature to draw any major conclusions about the implications of these differences. Further, we believe that the additional administrative requirements for non-physician prescribers within the direct-care system make it difficult for us to draw any strict comparisons between non-physician and physician prescribers without more information about those non-physician requirements.

Findings Regarding Purchased-Care System Prescribers

Within the purchased-care system, most prescribers have treated patients who have had their pharmacotherapy affected by either a formulary or a preferred-drug list. For example, 76 percent of purchased-care respondents indicated that more than a quarter of their patients have pharmacy benefits that were subject to formulary management, and 92 percent of purchased-care respondents reported that they prescribed medications based on formularies or preferred-drug lists in the previous three months.

Purchased-care prescribers reported being at least somewhat familiar with the content of these formularies or preferred-drug lists but less familiar with the rules and procedures governing non-formulary or non-preferred requests. However, many purchased-care respondents indicated having experience with multiple lists within the prior three months. Such exposure to multiple lists may have impacted their knowledge level as well as their opinions about formulary management practices in general.

Further, purchased-care prescribers were less likely than direct-care prescribers to believe that formularies assist in clinical decisionmaking and were less agreeable to the need to control health care costs through the use of formularies. They further noted that formularies are not up to date, and it is difficult to keep track of changes to them.

While almost half of the purchased-care respondents believed that patients can get non-formulary medications when the request is medically justified, they also reported denials of such requests more often than did the MTF prescribers we sampled.

We also noted some differences within the sample of purchased-care prescribers—for example between primary and secondary providers and between those with light TRICARE patient caseloads and those with heavy caseloads.

Based on our findings at this time and without additional multivariate analyses, we do not draw any major conclusions about what factors may predict these results. For example, the differences between analytic groups in the purchased-care system sample may be associated with other factors (e.g., amount of managed care participation) that were not assessed for this study.

Comparing the Direct-Care and Purchased-Care Samples

Acknowledging that the two samples were responding to two different systems, and that the questions in each survey were framed slightly differently (i.e., direct-care respondents were answering questions about the formulary at their current MTF, whereas purchased-care respondents were answering questions about their experiences with formularies more generally), it is nevertheless possible to make some comparisons about the opinions and attitudes of prescribers across the two systems.

As the findings described in Chapter 5 indicate, the practice styles of direct- and purchased-care prescribers are somewhat different. Network providers see a greater number of patients, spend a greater proportion of their time in direct patient care, and interact with multiple pharmacy benefit management systems. While MTF prescribers reported greater familiarity with formularies and had higher opinions of formulary management practices, it is likely that because private-sector providers deal with multiple, uncoordinated systems, their ability to stay informed on the formulary developments at each health plan is more limited.

MTF prescribers also appeared to be much closer to the current MTF formulary development and decisionmaking processes than were network prescribers (and were much more likely to be aware of the impact on MTF/DoD costs). Pharmacy management in the private sector is a relatively new practice (introduced over the past five to ten years), and it seems likely that most network providers have little contact with pharmacists or P&T committees, or have little input on formulary management decisions. There is also the possibility that MTF prescribers are inherently more comfortable with managed care techniques and environments than are the majority of purchased-care prescribers (i.e., private-sector physicians) in our survey, who avoid highly integrated environments such as the VA and staff HMOs (Glassman et al., 2001; William M. Mercer, Inc., 2001).

Direct-Care and Purchased-Care Prescribers' Areas of Consensus

Taken together, the surveys of direct-care and purchased-care prescribers yield some areas of consensus with regard to providers' perceptions about formularies and formulary management procedures. For example, we observed that the majority of respondents in both samples were at least somewhat familiar with the content of their respective formularies and the formulary management procedures they are asked to follow. In addition, prescribers in both systems reported having difficulty in keeping track of changes in formularies.

Prescribers in both systems also reported that they believed their patients could get access to non-formulary medications when it was medically justified. In both settings, prescribers had recent experiences requesting non-formulary medications. Differences were observed between the two systems, however, in the number of reported approvals of such requests. The direct-care prescribers reported that 96 percent of such requests were approved, compared with only 73 percent being approved in the purchased care system.[1]

Status of Follow-Up Survey Effort

In our original research design, we planned to conduct a follow-up survey six months after the Uniform Formulary was disseminated. Given the delay in the implementation of the UF, we are currently discussing the timing of the follow-up survey effort with the sponsoring office. (At the time of the survey, implementation was planned for October 2001; at the time of this writing, it is planned for mid-2003).

In the follow-up stage of this study, we will assess any changes in prescribers' attitudes and opinions of formulary management and examine prescribers' experiences with the UF itself. We also plan to conduct additional multivariate analyses of both the baseline and follow-up survey efforts to examine any differences by MHS health care service region, branch of service, and managed care support contractor.[2]

---

[1]Although these differences between systems could be tested using some assumptions, at the request of the sponsor, the additional programming and analyses required to do this testing were not pursued at this time.

[2]Managed care support contractors are the companies that manage the TRICARE program for the DoD within each of the health care service regions, of which there are currently four: TRIWest, HealthNet, Sierra, and Humana.

A. Survey Materials for Direct-Care Prescribers

In this appendix, we provide copies of materials used in this study that were sent to direct-care prescribers. Included are a copy of the "Survey on Medication Prescribing within Military Treatment Facilities"; a survey cover letter asking participants to share their experiences with, and opinions regarding, prescribing medications to patients who receive health care coverage through the MHS; three follow-up cover letters requesting participation in the survey; and the script used in a telephone follow-up to solicit prescribers' participation.

Department of Defense Military Health System

Survey on Medication Prescribing within Military Treatment Facilities

This survey has been designed to capture information about your experiences prescribing medications to outpatients within the Military Treatment Facility (MTF) to which you are currently assigned.

This survey is completely voluntary and RAND will keep all responses confidential, except as required by law. RAND will not give the Department of Defense any information that would link you to your responses. RAND will use the information you provide for health policy research purposes only.

Please note that all the questions in this survey refer to <u>YOUR ACTIVITIES WITHIN THE MTF</u> and not to patients you might see outside the MTF, for example on deployment.

Center for Military Health Policy Research
RAND
1200 South Hayes Street
Arlington, Virginia 22202-5050

> In this first section, we are interested in learning about your experiences writing outpatient prescriptions as an MTF provider and your familiarity with the formulary in use at your MTF.
>
> A <u>formulary</u> is a list of drugs covered under a patient's health benefits as well as the set of rules and procedures (including co-payments) governing the prescribing and obtaining of non-formulary drugs.

1. **On average, how many outpatients do you see per week at an MTF?** *Your best estimate is fine.*

   # OF OUTPATIENTS: ☐☐☐

2. **Approximately how many medications do you prescribe per week for these patients?** *Please include both new prescriptions and renewals.*

   (Check One)

   ₁ ☐ 20 or fewer outpatient prescriptions per week

   ₂ ☐ 21 to 40

   ₃ ☐ 41 to 60

   ₄ ☐ 61 to 80

   ₅ ☐ 81 to 100

   ₆ ☐ More than 100 outpatient prescriptions per week

3. **How do you know whether a drug you prescribe is included on your MTF's formulary?**

   (Check all that apply)

   ₁ ☐ I look at a printed or computerized formulary list

   ₂ ☐ I receive notice from an electronic prescribing menu in the physician order entry

   ₃ ☐ I receive feedback from the pharmacy or other sources

   ₄ ☐ My patients let me know

   ₅ ☐ I rely on my own memory

   ₆ ☐ Other *(please specify)*: _____

   ₈ ☐ Don't know

4. **In general, how familiar are you with:**   *(Check One Box on Each Line)*

	VERY FAMILIAR	SOMEWHAT FAMILIAR	NOT AT ALL FAMILIAR
a. The drugs that are listed on your MTF's formulary?	₁ ☐	₂ ☐	₃ ☐
b. The rules and procedures for prescribing drugs <u>not</u> on your MTF's formulary?	₁ ☐	₂ ☐	₃ ☐

1

5. In the <u>past 3 months</u>, how many times have you: *(Check One Box on Each Line)*

	NEVER	1 - 5 TIMES	6 - 10 TIMES	11 - 20 TIMES	MORE THAN 20 TIMES	DON'T KNOW
a. Changed the medication you originally prescribed because the drug was not on the MTF's formulary?	0 ☐	1 ☐	2 ☐	3 ☐	4 ☐	8 ☐
b. Considered prescribing a non-formulary drug but did not because you thought that the request would <u>be denied</u>?	0 ☐	1 ☐	2 ☐	3 ☐	4 ☐	8 ☐
c. Considered prescribing a non-formulary drug but did not because you thought that the process would <u>take too long</u>?	0 ☐	1 ☐	2 ☐	3 ☐	4 ☐	8 ☐
d. Advised patients to obtain a non-formulary drug outside of the MTF?	0 ☐	1 ☐	2 ☐	3 ☐	4 ☐	8 ☐
e. Been asked by a patient to prescribe a non-formulary drug even though you believed a formulary drug to be just as effective?	0 ☐	1 ☐	2 ☐	3 ☐	4 ☐	8 ☐
f. Been asked by a patient to re-write a prescription from a non-MTF provider in order for it to be filled at the MTF?	0 ☐	1 ☐	2 ☐	3 ☐	4 ☐	8 ☐
g. Been asked by a patient to prescribe a particular drug because the patient had seen it advertised?	0 ☐	1 ☐	2 ☐	3 ☐	4 ☐	8 ☐

6. In the <u>past 12 months</u>, how often did your patients complain to you about their out-of-pocket expenses (e.g. copayments) for their prescriptions?

(Check One)

0 ☐ Never

1 ☐ Seldom

2 ☐ Occasionally

3 ☐ Often

4 ☐ Very often

8 ☐ Don't know

7. Suppose a new patient has just moved to your MTF facility service area and is taking a non-formulary drug. Also, assume that a drug in the same therapeutic class is listed on the MTF formulary. In practice, which of the following would you be most likely to do first?
(Check One)

₁ ☐ I would convert the patient to a similar drug included on my MTF's formulary.

₂ ☐ I would request approval for the non-formulary drug to continue the prescription.

₃ ☐ I would advise the patient to obtain the drug outside the MTF.

₄ ☐ Other *(please specify)* _____

8. **Have you ever requested approval to prescribe a non-formulary drug?**
(Check One)

₁ ☐ Yes → *(Go to Question #9)*

₀ ☐ No → *(Go to Question #13)*

9. **For routine requests for approval to prescribe a non-formulary drug, how long does it generally take for you to learn whether or not your request has been approved?**
(Check One)

₀ ☐ Less than 1 day

₁ ☐ 1 to 2 days

₂ ☐ 3 to 5 days

₃ ☐ More than 5 days

₈ ☐ Don't know

10. **In the past 3 months:**

a. How many times did you request approval to prescribe a non-formulary drug? *Your best estimate is fine.*
(IF 'NEVER,' WRITE IN '00' AND GO TO QUESTION #13)

OF REQUESTS: ☐☐ **OR** ₈ ☐ Don't Know

b. How many times were these requests <u>denied</u>?
Your best estimate is fine.
(IF 'NEVER,' WRITE IN '00' AND GO TO QUESTION #12)

DENIED: ☐☐ **OR** ₈ ☐ Don't Know

11. Think about the **most recent case** for which your request for a non-formulary drug was **denied**:

   a. **Which of the following actions did you take?**

   (Check All That Apply)

   ₁ ☐ I appealed the denial.

   ₂ ☐ I resubmitted the request with more information.

   ₃ ☐ I sought approval of a different non-formulary drug.

   ₄ ☐ I prescribed a formulary drug.

   ₅ ☐ I advised the patient to obtain the non-formulary drug outside the MTF.

   ₆ ☐ Other *(please specify):* _____

   ₈ ☐ Can't remember

   b. **How was the patient's health affected as a result of not getting the non-formulary drug you initially requested?**

   (Check One)

   ₁ ☐ It's too soon to tell.

   ₂ ☐ The patient's health was unaffected.

   ₃ ☐ The patient experienced a <u>minor</u> decline in health status.

   ₄ ☐ The patient experienced a <u>major</u> decline in health status.

   ₅ ☐ Other *(please specify):* _____

   ₈ ☐ Don't know / Can't remember

12. **In the past 3 months, how many times have you:**   *(Check One Box on Each Line)*

	NEVER	1 - 5 TIMES	6 - 10 TIMES	11 - 20 TIMES	MORE THAN 20 TIMES	DON'T KNOW
a. Requested approval for a non-formulary drug originally prescribed outside the MTF because the patients wanted to fill the prescription at the MTF?	₀ ☐	₁ ☐	₂ ☐	₃ ☐	₄ ☐	₈ ☐
b. Requested approval to prescribe a non-formulary drug because a patient requested it, even though you believed that another drug on the formulary would have been just as effective?	₀ ☐	₁ ☐	₂ ☐	₃ ☐	₄ ☐	₈ ☐

The following items ask for your personal opinions on a number of issues that may affect day-to-day clinical practice within the MTF.

13. **With regard to the patients seeking care at your MTF, how strongly do you agree or disagree with the following statements:** *(Check One Box on Each Line)*

	STRONGLY AGREE	AGREE	NEITHER AGREE NOR DISAGREE	DISAGREE	STRONGLY DISAGREE
a. Patients filling prescriptions written by outside providers drain resources from my MTF.	1☐	2☐	3☐	4☐	5☐
b. Re-writing prescriptions that originate from outside to be filled at the MTF is burdensome to prescribers at my facility.	1☐	2☐	3☐	4☐	5☐
c. Direct-to-consumer advertisement prompts my patients to seek care for health conditions that might otherwise go untreated.	1☐	2☐	3☐	4☐	5☐
d. Patients' requests for advertised drugs make my job more challenging.	1☐	2☐	3☐	4☐	5☐

14. **With regard to the formulary at your MTF, how strongly do you agree or disagree with the following statements:** *(Check One Box on Each Line)*

	STRONGLY AGREE	AGREE	NEITHER AGREE NOR DISAGREE	DISAGREE	STRONGLY DISAGREE
a. It is easy to keep track of changes made to the list of drugs on my MTF's formulary.	1☐	2☐	3☐	4☐	5☐
b. The MTF's formulary has done a good job keeping drugs up-to-date in the drug classes I would like to prescribe.	1☐	2☐	3☐	4☐	5☐
c. The MTF's formulary helps my ability to prescribe clinically appropriate drugs.	1☐	2☐	3☐	4☐	5☐
d. It is important for the MTF to save money, when possible, by choosing the drug with the best value within a therapeutic class.	1☐	2☐	3☐	4☐	5☐
e. My MTF patients can obtain non-formulary drugs when medically justified.	1☐	2☐	3☐	4☐	5☐
f. The drug restrictions imposed by the MTF's formulary are a necessary component for containing costs.	1☐	2☐	3☐	4☐	5☐
g. Overall, I am satisfied with the non-formulary waiver / approval process in my MTF.	1☐	2☐	3☐	4☐	5☐

5

The next several questions ask about your familiarity with, opinion of, and recommendations on the processes and policies that govern the composition of your MTF formulary. For your reference, the MTF's Pharmacy & Therapeutics (P&T) Committee is the oversight committee which decides what drugs will be covered by the MTF's formulary. The P&T Committee also establishes policies and procedures governing access to restricted and non-formulary drugs.

15. **How familiar are you with the activities of your MTF's Pharmacy & Therapeutics Committee?**

    (Check One)

    1 ☐ Very familiar

    2 ☐ Somewhat familiar

    3 ☐ Not at all familiar → *(Go to Question #17)*

16. **How strongly do you agree or disagree with the following statements:**

                                                                    (Check One Box on Each Line)

	STRONGLY AGREE	AGREE	NEITHER AGREE NOR DISAGREE	DISAGREE	STRONGLY DISAGREE
a. The MTF's Pharmacy & Therapeutics (P&T) Committee is responsive to the concerns of providers.	1 ☐	2 ☐	3 ☐	4 ☐	5 ☐
b. I have confidence in the ability of the MTF's P&T Committee to choose for use at my facility the safest and most clinically effective drugs.	1 ☐	2 ☐	3 ☐	4 ☐	5 ☐
c. I have confidence in the ability of the MTF's P&T Committee to choose for use at my facility the drugs with the best value.	1 ☐	2 ☐	3 ☐	4 ☐	5 ☐
d. Overall, I am satisfied with the decisions and actions of my MTF's 'P&T Committee.	1 ☐	2 ☐	3 ☐	4 ☐	5 ☐

17. **What would make it easier for MTF providers to comply with the MTF's formulary?**

    (Check All That Apply)

    ₁ ☐ Feedback on their prescribing patterns

    ₂ ☐ Regular reminders on content of the formulary

    ₃ ☐ Electronic prescribing

    ₄ ☐ Regularly updated formulary lists

    ₅ ☐ Web-based formulary lists for easy access

    ₆ ☐ Better responsiveness to providers concerns regarding formulary content, policies and procedures

    ₇ ☐ Other *(please specify):* _____

    ₈ ☐ Don't know

18. **If you had the opportunity, what changes would you make to the content, policies and/or procedures of your MTF's formulary?**

    _____

    _____

    _____

    _____

    _____

    _____

    _____

    _____

    _____

    _____

    _____

    _____

19. In a typical workweek, how many hours do you spend working at an MTF? *Your best estimate is fine.*

OF HOURS: ☐☐☐

20. On average, what percentage of your time per week do you spend doing each of the following professional activities at an MTF? *Your best estimate is fine.*

% OF TIME PER WEEK

a. Management or administration .... ☐☐☐ %

b. Seeing patients (either by yourself or accompanied by other providers) .... ☐☐☐ %

c. Teaching activities (i.e. giving lectures or clinical tutorials)................................. ☐☐☐ %

d. Research .... ☐☐☐ %

e. Readiness .... ☐☐☐ %

f. Other professional activities .... ☐☐☐ %

    *(please specify):*_____

TOTAL 100%

21. In what type of setting do you see (either by yourself or accompanied by other providers) <u>most</u> of your MTF patients?

(Check One)

1 ☐ Outpatient clinic

2 ☐ Hospital inpatient setting

3 ☐ Other *(please specify)* _____

22. What is your <u>*primary*</u> discipline?

(Check One)

1 ☐ Physician ➝ *(Go to Question #23)*

2 ☐ Advanced practice nurse ➝ *(Go to Question #24)*

3 ☐ Physician assistant ➝ *(Go to Question #24)*

4 ☐ Other *(please specify)* _____

_____ ➝ *(Go to Question #24)*

8

23. If you are a physician, what is your current status?
(Check One)

1 ☐ Attending

2 ☐ Fellow

3 ☐ Intern

4 ☐ Resident

5 ☐ Other *(please specify)* _____

24. What is your *primary* area of specialty?
(Check One)

1 ☐ Family Practice/Family Medicine

2 ☐ Geriatrics

3 ☐ General Internal Medicine

4 ☐ Internal Medicine subspecialty *(please specify)* _____

5 ☐ Obstetrics & Gynecology

6 ☐ Pediatrics

7 ☐ Dermatology

8 ☐ Other *(please specify)* _____

25. Approximately, how many months or years have you worked at:

a. The MTF to which you are currently assigned?.................................. MONTHS: ☐☐ YEARS: ☐☐

b. Other MTFs (excluding the one to which
you are currently assigned)?.. MONTHS: ☐☐ YEARS: ☐☐

26. What is your current military pay grade?
(Check One)

1 ☐ O-1

2 ☐ O-2

3 ☐ O-3

4 ☐ O-4

5 ☐ O-5

6 ☐ O-6

7 ☐ Not applicable

27. Are you currently:

(Check All That Apply)

₁ ☐ Active Duty Personnel

₂ ☐ Reservist

₃ ☐ Civilian

₄ ☐ Other *(please specify)* _____

28. How old were you on your last birthday?   AGE: ☐☐

Do you have any other comments?

_____
_____
_____
_____
_____
_____
_____
_____
_____
_____
_____
_____

Please return your completed survey to RAND in the pre-paid return envelope provided.

Please do <u>not</u> write your name or address anywhere on the questionnaire or the return envelope.

If you have any other questions or if you are missing your return envelope, please call this toll-free number: 1-866-456-1518.

THANK YOU FOR YOUR TIME

DATE

<FIRST NAMES> <LAST NAME>

<ADDRESS 1>

<ADDRESS 2>

<CITY>, <STATE> <ZIP>

Dear <TITLE> <LAST NAME>:

Your assistance is urgently needed! Congress has directed the Assistant Secretary of Defense to evaluate the pharmacy benefits program for patients within the Military Health System (MHS). To this end, the Department of Defense (DoD) has asked RAND, an independent non-profit research organization with extensive experience studying health care systems, to conduct a confidential survey of health care providers who treat MHS beneficiaries.

As a health care provider to MHS beneficiaries receiving care at Military Treatment Facilities (MTFs), you have been randomly selected to participate in this study. The aim of this survey is to learn more about your experiences prescribing medication within your MTF. *Your response to this survey will help the DoD better understand how to improve the prescription benefits it offers to military personnel and their families.*

Enclosed please find a self-administered questionnaire for you to complete and return in the postage-paid envelope as soon as possible. We want to assure you that your participation in this study is *completely voluntary* and that RAND will keep all of your responses *strictly confidential*, except as required by law. While RAND will provide the DoD with a file containing the responses to this questionnaire, RAND will remove, prior to sharing the data with the DoD, all data from the file that would allow for the identification of any specific individual or health care facility. If you have any questions or concerns regarding this study, please call RAND toll-free at 866-456-1518.

I thank you in advance for your participation in this important study.

Sincerely,

Peter A. Glassman, MBBS, MSc

Study Principal Investigator

94

DATE

<FIRST NAME> <LAST NAME>

<ADDRESS 1>

<ADDRESS 2>

<CITY>, <STATE> <ZIP>

Dear <TITLE> <LAST NAME>:

Your assistance is urgently needed! In the past week, you should have received in the mail a questionnaire with a blue cover titled **Survey on Medication Prescribing within Military Treatment Facilities**.

This confidential survey of health care providers who treat military health system beneficiaries is being conducted by RAND, an independent non-profit research organization, on behalf of the Assistant Secretary of Defense. This letter is to remind you to take a few minutes to complete and return your questionnaire. If you have already done so, thanks and please disregard this letter.

In the questionnaire packet recently sent to you, a postage-paid envelope was included. Please use this envelope to return your completed questionnaire. If you no longer have this envelope, if you have misplaced your questionnaire, or if you never received the questionnaire in the mail, just call 1-866-456-1518 and another one will be sent to you. Also, if you have any questions or concerns regarding this study, please do not hesitate to call Ana Suarez at this toll-free number.

Thank you again for your time and assistance in this important study.

Sincerely,

Peter A. Glassman, MBBS, MSc

Study Principal Investigator

<DATE>

<TITLE> <FIRST NAMES> <LAST NAME>

<ADDRESS 1>

<ADDRESS 2>

<CITY>, <STATE> <ZIP>

Dear <TITLE> <LAST NAME>:

Your input is still needed! I am writing to you once again to urge you to take a few minutes to complete the enclosed questionnaire on medication prescribing. You were selected as part of a national sample of health care providers who treat beneficiaries of the Military Health System (MHS).

This is important and timely research. Your response will enable the Department of Defense's (DoD) TRICARE Management Activity to consider your experience and opinions in managing pharmacy benefits for patients receiving health care coverage through the Military Health System.

The Assistant Secretary of Defense asked RAND, a private non-profit research organization, to administer this survey. I want to assure you that your participation in this study is *completely voluntary* and that RAND will keep all of your responses confidential, except as required by law. The DoD will not have access to any responses that might identify you or your healthcare facility.

Again, this is a very important study in light of upcoming changes to health care and pharmacy coverage for MHS beneficiaries. By participating in this survey, you can assist DoD's TRICARE Management Activity in determining how these changes might affect you and your ability to effectively provide quality care for your MHS patients.

If you have already responded to this request, I thank you for your time. If you have not, I would appreciate if you could please do so as soon as possible. We have included a postage-paid envelope for your convenience.

Should you have any questions, please feel free to contact Ana Suarez at RAND. She can be reached toll free at 1-866-456-1518.

Thank you.

Sincerely,

Peter A. Glassman, MBBS, MSc

Study Principal Investigator

<DATE>

<TITLE> <FIRST NAMES> <LAST NAME>

<ADDRESS 1>

<ADDRESS 2>

<CITY>, <STATE> <ZIP>

Dear <TITLE> <LAST NAME>:

Your input is still needed! I am writing a final letter to again urge you to tell us about your experiences with and opinions regarding prescribing medications to patients who receive health care coverage through the Military Health System (MHS). If you have already sent back your survey, thank you. If you would like to have your voice heard, please complete and return the enclosed questionnaire *as soon as possible*. A postage-paid envelope is enclosed for your convenience.

This is important and timely research *in light of upcoming changes to health care and pharmacy coverage for MHS beneficiaries.* Your response will enable the Department of Defense's (DoD) TRICARE Management Activity to better understand how these changes might affect the ability of clinicians, like yourself, to effectively provide quality care for their MHS patients.

The Assistant Secretary of Defense asked RAND, a private non-profit research organization, to administer this survey. You were selected as part of a national sample of health care providers at military treatment facilities who treat beneficiaries of the MHS. I want to assure you that your participation in this study is *completely voluntary* and that RAND will keep all of your responses confidential, except as required by law. DoD will not have access to any responses that might identify you or your health care facility.

Should you have any questions, please feel free to contact Ana Suarez at RAND. She can be reached toll free at 1-866-456-1518.

Thank you!

Sincerely,

Peter A. Glassman, MBBS, MSc

Study Principal Investigator

DOD FORMULARY SURVEY

FOLLOW-UP PROMPTING

TELEPHONE SCRIPT FOR MTF SAMPLE

IF YOU REACH A RECORDING:

1. **BASED ON THE GREETING, TRY TO VERIFY THAT YOU HAVE REACHED THE FACILITY/OFFICE OF RESPONDENT.**

1 YES – **TRY AGAIN LATER**

2 NO – **CODE AS 'PROB'**

3 NOT SURE – **TRY AGAIN LATER; MAKE NOTE UNDER "COMMENTS"**

IF A PERSON ANSWERS:

2. Hello, my name is _____, and I'm calling from RAND, a research organization in <Santa Monica, California OR Arlington, VA>.

    IF NEEDED: Have I reached <HEALTH FACILITY>?

    a. REACHED R's FACILITY- **GO TO #3**

    b. DID NOT REACH R's FACILITY - **VERIFY NUMBER; IF WRONG NUMBER, CODE AS 'WN' AND BRING TO THE ATTENTION OF SUPERVISOR.**

3.

    a. I'm trying to reach <RESPONDENT>. Does he/she work at this health facility?

    IF R IS AT THIS FACILITY: Could I please speak with <RESPONDENT>?

    a. R AT THIS FACILITY AND R IS AVAILABLE - **GO TO #6**

    b. R AT THIS FACILITY BUT R IS NOT AVAILABLE AT THIS TIME – **GO TO #4**

    c. R DOES NOT WORK AT THIS FACILITY (ANYMORE) – **FIND OUT WHEN R LEFT THE FACILITY; GO TO #13 AND CODE AS 'OA'**

    d. DO NOT KNOW – **GO TO #13 AND CODE AS 'PROB'**

4.   When would be a good time to reach <RESPONDENT>?

        ENTER DATE/TIME ON CALL RECORDS

        a.   DATE/TIME SPECIFIED – **GO TO #5 AND CODE AS 'SCB.' INDICATE DATE & TIME GIVEN**

        b.   NO SPECIFIC TIME – **GO TO #5 AND CODE AS 'SCB'**

5.   May I leave a message for <RESPONDENT>?

        IF LEAVING A MESSAGE WITH A PERSON:

        My name is _____ and I'm calling from RAND, a non-profit research organization, regarding a questionnaire we mailed to him/her for a study we are conducting on behalf of the Department of Defense. I would appreciate it if <R> could call me back toll free at (866) 456-1518.

        IF LEAVING A MESSAGE ON VOICEMAIL:

        This message is for <RESPONDENT>. My name is _____, and I'm calling from RAND, a non-profit research organization, regarding a study we are conducting on behalf of the Department of Defense. We recently sent you a questionnaire and I'm calling to find out if you received it. I would appreciate it if you could call me back at your earliest convenience. The toll free number is (866) 456-1518 and again, my name is _____. I will also follow up with you soon if you are unable to return my call. I want to thank you in advance for your participation in this study.

1.   LEFT MESSAGE – **GO TO #13 (if needed) AND CODE AS 'LM-P' OR 'LM-AM'**

2.   UNABLE TO LEAVE MESSAGE – **GO TO #13**

IF RESPONDENT COMES ON LINE:

6.   Hello, my name is _____, and I'm calling from RAND, a non-profit research organization, regarding a study of prescribers we are conducting on behalf of the Department of Defense. We recently sent you a questionnaire asking you about your experiences prescribing medications and I'm calling to find out if you received the questionnaire.

IF NEEDED: The study packet was first mailed to you in early April and then again at the beginning of May. It included a questionnaire and a cover letter explaining the study.

IF NEEDED: This study is part of an extensive effort by the U.S. Department of Defense to improve the quality of the healthcare being provided to military personnel and their families. However, this study is not designed to evaluate individual healthcare providers or health facilities. It simply aims at finding out more about how, in general, military health beneficiaries receive their prescriptions from their providers and the provider's experience prescribing medications to them.

Participation is completely voluntary, and RAND will keep all of your responses strictly confidential. Please be assured that RAND will not release any information that can be linked to an individual or a facility. Even though the Department of Defense is sponsoring this survey, RAND is working independently. Therefore, your identity is protected.

The success of the study depends on our obtaining a representative sample of health care providers serving military health beneficiaries, so your participation is extremely important. You were selected at random from a national pool of health care providers who treat military health beneficiaries. It should only take you about 15 minutes to complete the questionnaire. We hope we can count on your help.

a. RECEIVED QUESTIONNAIRE AND ALREADY RETURNED IT – **GO TO #13 AND CODE AS 'RC'**

b. RECEIVED QUESTIONNAIRE BUT DIDN'T COMPLETE IT YET - **GO TO #7**

c. STUDY NOT APPLICABLE TO R – **GO TO #8**

d. NEEDS REMAIL – **GO TO #9 AND CODE AS 'RM'**

e. REFUSAL - **GO TO #10**

IF RESPONDENT RECEIVED QUESTIONNAIRE:

    a.   When might you be able to return the questionnaire?

IF NEEDED: We would appreciate it if you could complete it as soon as possible since we are scheduled to complete data collection in June in order to meet the deadline for reporting the results of the study to Congress.

    1 WILL RETURN – ENTER DATE ON CALL RECORD – **GO TO #12 AND CODE AS 'WC'**

    2 REFUSAL - **GO TO #10**

QUESTIONNAIRE NOT APPLICABLE TO R

    a.   You were selected for this study based on information we received from the TRICARE Management Activity at the Department of Defense, which indicated that you have prescribing privileges at your facility. Can you prescribe medications to the patients you treat?

    1   IF YES – **GO BACK TO OUTCOMES IN #6 AND FOLLOW SCRIPT FOR OUTCOMES #2, #4 OR #5, ACCORDINGLY**

    2   IF DOESN'T PRESCRIBE MEDICATIONS OR DOESN'T TREAT PATIENTS –
I will make a note of this on our records so that we do not send you any more surveys.
GO TO #13 AND CODE AS 'NE'

REMAIL:

9.   I can re-send the study packet to you. We would appreciate it if you complete it and return it as soon as possible since we are scheduled to complete data collection in June in order to meet the deadline for reporting the results of the study to Congress. Let me confirm your mailing address.

a.   THE FACILITY ADDRESS ON FILE VERIFIED - **GO TO # 12**

b.   CHANGES TO THE FACILITY ADDRESS ON FILE – **GO TO #12**

REFUSAL:

10.   Your participation is critical in order for the results of this study to be as representative as possible of all prescribers who treat military health beneficiaries. We expect the results to be very useful to health care providers, administrators, and policymakers within the Military Health System. It should only take you about 15 minutes to complete the survey. I can assure you, we will not share any identifiable information about individuals or their facilities.

a. STILL REFUSES – **GO TO #11**
b. OBJECTIONS OVERCOME – NEEDS ANOTHER COPY OF SURVEY – **GO TO #9 AND CODE AS 'RM'**
            OBJECTIONS OVERCOME – HAS SURVEY – **GO TO #12 AND CODE AS 'WC'**

11.   I am sorry that you do not wish to participate in this study. May I ask why?

        IF NEEDED: Knowing why a prescriber can not or does not wish to participate in this study will help us better understand if, and how, those who do not participate differ from those who do.

GO TO #13, CODE AS 'R-NI' AND INDICATE REASON GIVEN IF ANY

IF RESPONDENT SAYS HE/SHE WILL COMPLETE QUESTIONNAIRE:

12. We really appreciate you taking the time to participate in this survey. The study packet includes a self-addressed and stamped envelope for you to return the questionnaire. There is no need for you to write your name or address anywhere on the questionnaire. Please be assured that RAND will keep all of your responses strictly confidential and that RAND will not make your responses public in any way that can be linked to you directly or your facility.

        GO TO #13

13.   **CLOSING:**
        Thank you very much.

        (CODE OUTCOME AND NOTES ON CALL RECORD)

B. Survey Materials for Purchased-Care Prescribers

In this appendix, we provide copies of materials used in this study that were sent to purchased-care prescribers. Included (in this order) are a copy of the "Survey on Medication Prescribing and Prescription Drug Benefits"; a survey cover letter asking participants to share their experiences with prescribing medications to their patients in general and to TRICARE patients in particular; a follow-up cover letter requesting participation in the survey; a cover sheet used to get the recipient's attention that was inserted on top of the third follow-up mailing packet; the third follow-up cover letter; and the script used in a telephone follow-up to solicit prescribers' participation.

Department of Defense Military Health System

Survey on Medication Prescribing and Prescription Drug Benefits

---

You were selected to receive this survey as a managed care support contractor under the Department of Defense (DoD) TRICARE program. This survey has been designed to capture information about your experiences prescribing medications to outpatients and your opinions regarding prescription drug benefits.

This survey is completely voluntary and RAND will keep all responses confidential, except as required by law. RAND will not give DoD any information that would link you to your responses. RAND will use the information you provide for health policy research purposes only.

Center for Military Health Policy Research
RAND
1200 South Hayes Street
Arlington, Virginia 22202-5050

OMB Control: 0720-0024 Expiration Date: 6/30/2003

In this first section, we are interested in learning about your overall experience writing outpatient prescriptions for ALL of your patients, not just your TRICARE patients.

1. **On average, how many <u>outpatients</u> do you see per week?** *Please think about all of your patients, not just your TRICARE patients. Your best estimate is fine.*

   # OF OUTPATIENTS: ☐☐☐

2. **Approximately how many medications do you prescribe per week for these <u>outpatients</u>?** *Please include both new prescriptions and renewals.*

   (Check One Only)

   1 ☐ None

   2 ☐ 1 to 20 outpatient prescriptions per week

   3 ☐ 21 to 40

   4 ☐ 41 to 60

   5 ☐ 61 to 80

   6 ☐ 81 to 100

   7 ☐ More than 100 outpatient prescriptions per week

THE NEXT QUESTIONS IN THIS SECTION INQUIRE ABOUT YOUR EXPOSURE TO FORMULARIES AND PREFERRED DRUG LISTS:

A <u>formulary</u> is a list of drugs covered by a patient's health insurance plan as well as a set of rules and procedures for obtaining medically indicated drugs not covered on the formulary list (i.e. non-formulary drugs).

A <u>preferred drug list</u> contains drugs that require lower patient co-payments compared to drugs not included on the list (i.e. non-preferred drugs). In many cases, physicians must request a waiver before a patient can obtain medically indicated non-preferred drugs at the lower co-payment rate.

3. **In the <u>past 3 months</u>, have you prescribed medications for outpatients whose drug benefits are based on either formularies <u>or</u> preferred drug lists?**

   (Check One Only)

   1 ☐ Yes → *(Go to Question #4, next page)*

   0 ☐ No → *(Skip to page 7, Question #17)*

   8 ☐ Don't know → *(Skip to page 7, Question #17)*

4. How many different <u>formulary lists</u> have you encountered over the <u>past 3 months</u>? *(Check One Only)*

   ₁ ☐ None → *(Skip to Question #7 on this page)*

   ₂ ☐ 1 to 2 formulary lists

   ₃ ☐ 3 to 5 formulary lists ⟶ *(Go to Question #5 on this page)*

   ₄ ☐ More than 5 formulary lists

5. How familiar are you with: *(Check One Box on Each Line)*

	VERY FAMILIAR	SOMEWHAT FAMILIAR	NOT AT ALL FAMILIAR
a. The drugs that are included on these <u>formularies</u>?	₁ ☐	₂ ☐	₃ ☐
b. The rules and procedures for prescribing <u>non-formulary</u> drugs?	₁ ☐	₂ ☐	₃ ☐

6. Please estimate the percentage of your <u>outpatients</u> that are covered by these <u>formularies</u>: *(Check One Only)*

   ₁ ☐ None

   ₂ ☐ Less than 10%

   ₃ ☐ 10% to 24%

   ₄ ☐ 25% to 50%

   ₅ ☐ More than 50%

   ₈ ☐ Don't know

7. How many different <u>preferred drug lists</u> have you encountered over the <u>past 3 months</u>? *(Check One Only)*

   ₁ ☐ None → *(Skip to Question #10, next page)*

   ₂ ☐ 1 to 2 preferred drug lists

   ₃ ☐ 3 to 5 preferred drug lists ⟶ *(Go to Question #8 on this page)*

   ₄ ☐ More than 5 preferred drug lists

8. How familiar are you with: *(Check One Box on Each Line)*

	VERY FAMILIAR	SOMEWHAT FAMILIAR	NOT AT ALL FAMILIAR
a. The drugs that are included on these <u>preferred drug lists</u>?	₁ ☐	₂ ☐	₃ ☐
b. The rules and procedures for prescribing <u>non-preferred</u> drugs?	₁ ☐	₂ ☐	₃ ☐

OMB Control: 0720-0024
Expiration Date: 6/30/2003

9. Please estimate the percentage of your outpatients that are covered by these __preferred drug lists__:

(Check One Only)

1 ☐ None

2 ☐ Less than 10%

3 ☐ 10% to 24%

4 ☐ 25% to 50%

5 ☐ More than 50%

8 ☐ Don't know

THE REMAINING QUESTIONS IN THIS SECTION REFER TO BOTH FORMULARIES __AND__ PREFERRED DRUG LISTS. ALTHOUGH THE TWO ARE NOT EXACTLY THE SAME, THE RULES AND PROCEDURES FOR OBTAINING NON-FORMULARY DRUGS APPLY IN MANY INSTANCES. WE ARE INTERESTED IN HOW THESE RULES AND PROCEDURES AFFECT YOUR PRACTICE IN GENERAL.

10. In the __past 3 months__, how many times have you: *(Check One Box on Each Line)*

	NEVER	1 - 5 TIMES	6 - 10 TIMES	11 - 20 TIMES	MORE THAN 20 TIMES	DON'T KNOW
a. changed the medication you originally prescribed because the drug was not on the patient's health plan formulary/list of preferred drugs?	0 ☐	1 ☐	2 ☐	3 ☐	4 ☐	8 ☐
b. considered prescribing a non-formulary/non-preferred drug but did not because you thought that the request would <u>be denied</u>?	0 ☐	1 ☐	2 ☐	3 ☐	4 ☐	8 ☐
c. considered prescribing a non-formulary/non-preferred drug but did not because you thought that the process would <u>take too long</u>?	0 ☐	1 ☐	2 ☐	3 ☐	4 ☐	8 ☐
d. been asked by a patient to prescribe a non-formulary/non-preferred drug even though you believed the formulary/preferred drug to be just as effective?	0 ☐	1 ☐	2 ☐	3 ☐	4 ☐	8 ☐
e. requested approval to prescribe a non-formulary/non-preferred drug because a patient requested it, even though you believed that another drug on the formulary would have been just as effective?	0 ☐	1 ☐	2 ☐	3 ☐	4 ☐	8 ☐
f. been asked by a patient to prescribe a particular drug because the patient had seen it advertised?	0 ☐	1 ☐	2 ☐	3 ☐	4 ☐	8 ☐

11. Have you <u>ever</u> requested approval to prescribe a non-formulary/non-preferred drug?

(Check One Only)

   ₁ ☐ Yes → *(Go to Question #12 on this page)*

   ₀ ☐ No → *(Skip to Question #14, next page)*

12. In the <u>past 3 months</u>:

a. How many times did you request approval to prescribe a non-formulary/non-preferred drug? *Your best estimate is fine.* *(If 'never,' write in '00' and skip to Question #14, next page)*

   # OF REQUESTS: ☐☐   **OR**   ₈ ☐ Don't Know

b. How many times were these requests <u>denied</u>? *Your best estimate is fine.* *(If 'never,' write in '00' and skip to Question #14, next page)*

   # DENIED: ☐☐   **OR**   ₈ ☐ Don't Know

13. Think about the <u>most recent case</u> for which your request for a non-formulary/non-preferred drug was <u>denied</u>:

a. **Which of the following actions did you take?**

(Check All That Apply)

   ₁ ☐ I appealed the denial.

   ₂ ☐ I resubmitted the request with more information.

   ₃ ☐ I sought approval of a different non-formulary / non-preferred drug.

   ₄ ☐ I prescribed a formulary / preferred drug.

   ₅ ☐ Other *(please specify):* _____

   ₈ ☐ Can't remember

b. **How was the patient's health affected as a result of not getting the non-formulary/non-preferred drug you initially requested?**

(Check One Only)

   ₁ ☐ It's too soon to tell.

   ₂ ☐ The patient's health was unaffected.

   ₃ ☐ The patient experienced a <u>minor</u> decline in health status.

   ₄ ☐ The patient experienced a <u>major</u> decline in health status.

   ₅ ☐ Other *(please specify):* _____

   ₈ ☐ Don't know / Can't remember

OMB Control: 0720-0024
Expiration Date: 6/30/2003

This section asks for your opinion regarding drug formularies, including their content and governing procedures and policies, as well as their impact on day-to-day clinical practice. For your reference, a Pharmacy and Therapeutics (P&T) Committee is the oversight committee which decides what drugs will be covered by a formulary or preferred list, and establishes the policies and procedures governing access to non-formulary/non-preferred drugs.

14. How strongly do you agree or disagree with the following statements:

(Check One Box on Each Line)

	STRONGLY AGREE	AGREE	NEITHER AGREE NOR DISAGREE	DISAGREE	STRONGLY DISAGREE
a. It is easy to keep track of changes made to these formularies/lists of preferred drugs.	1 ☐	2 ☐	3 ☐	4 ☐	5 ☐
b. These formularies/lists of preferred drugs have done a good job keeping drugs up-to-date in the drug classes I would like to prescribe.	1 ☐	2 ☐	3 ☐	4 ☐	5 ☐
c. These formularies/lists of preferred drugs help my ability to prescribe clinically appropriate drugs.	1 ☐	2 ☐	3 ☐	4 ☐	5 ☐
d. It is important for health plans to save money by choosing for their formularies/list of preferred drugs the drug with the best value within its therapeutic class.	1 ☐	2 ☐	3 ☐	4 ☐	5 ☐
e. My patients can obtain non-formulary / non-preferred drugs when medically justified.	1 ☐	2 ☐	3 ☐	4 ☐	5 ☐
f. The drug restrictions imposed by these formularies / lists of preferred drugs are a necessary component for containing costs in a health plan.	1 ☐	2 ☐	3 ☐	4 ☐	5 ☐
g. Pharmacy & Therapeutics (P&T) Committees are responsive to the concerns of providers.	1 ☐	2 ☐	3 ☐	4 ☐	5 ☐
h. I have confidence in the ability of P&T Committees to choose the safest and most clinically effective drugs.	1 ☐	2 ☐	3 ☐	4 ☐	5 ☐
i. I have confidence in the ability of P&T Committees to choose the drugs with the best value.	1 ☐	2 ☐	3 ☐	4 ☐	5 ☐

15. Which of the following statements best describes what you currently do in your daily practice to determine which drugs have been included in a formulary or a preferred drug list under a patient's health plan?

(Check One Only)

1 ☐ I look at a written formulary or preferred drug list from the patient's insurer/health plan.

2 ☐ I go to the website of the patient's insurer/health plan.

3 ☐ I know by memory most of the common drugs that are covered by my patients' insurers/health plans.

4 ☐ I write what I think is on the formulary/preferred drug list and assume that a pharmacist will call me if it is not.

5 ☐ If I don't know, then I ask my staff to find out if a drug is covered.

6 ☐ I think that it is the patient's responsibility to determine whether a drug is on a formulary or a preferred drug list and to let me know if it is not.

7 ☐ Other method *(please specify):*_____

16. What would make it easier for providers to comply with a formulary/list of preferred drugs?

(Check All That Apply)

1 ☐ Feedback on their prescribing patterns

2 ☐ Regular reminders on content of formulary

3 ☐ Electronic prescribing

4 ☐ Regularly updated formulary list

5 ☐ Web-based formulary list for easy access

6 ☐ Better responsiveness to providers concerns regarding formulary content, policies and procedures

7 ☐ Other *(please specify):* _____

8 ☐ Don't know

OMB Control: 0720-0024
Expiration Date: 6/30/2003

Please tell us your opinion regarding direct-to-consumer advertisement of and tiered co-payment systems for prescription drugs.

17. How strongly do you agree or disagree with the following statements:

(Check One Box on Each Line)

	STRONGLY AGREE	AGREE	NEITHER AGREE NOR DISAGREE	DISAGREE	STRONGLY DISAGREE
a. Direct-to-consumer advertisement prompts my patients to seek care for health conditions that might otherwise go untreated.	1 ☐	2 ☐	3 ☐	4 ☐	5 ☐
b. Patients' requests for advertised drugs make my job more challenging.	1 ☐	2 ☐	3 ☐	4 ☐	5 ☐
c. A tiered co-payment system, in which a patient pays more for non-formulary/non-preferred drugs, promotes cost-effective prescribing.	1 ☐	2 ☐	3 ☐	4 ☐	5 ☐
d. A tiered co-payment system, as described in Q17c above, places an unfair burden on patients.	1 ☐	2 ☐	3 ☐	4 ☐	5 ☐
e. A tiered co-payment system, as described in Q17c above, limits the effect of drug advertising.	1 ☐	2 ☐	3 ☐	4 ☐	5 ☐

As you know, you were sampled for this survey because you have provided treatment services to military beneficiaries under a TRICARE managed care support contract. The questions in this section inquire about your professional practice as it relates to TRICARE beneficiaries.

18. Which of the following best describes your contractual arrangement to treat TRICARE patients?

(Check One Only)

1 ☐ TRICARE Prime

2 ☐ TRICARE Extra

3 ☐ TRICARE Standard

4 ☐ Other *(please specify)*: _____

8 ☐ Don't know

19. **How long have you been treating TRICARE patients?**

   (Check One Only)

   1 ☐ Less than a year

   2 ☐ 1 to 5 years

   3 ☐ More than 5 years

   8 ☐ Don't know

20. **Approximately what percent of your outpatients are TRICARE patients?**

   (Check One Only)

   1 ☐ Less than 10%

   2 ☐ 10% to 24%

   3 ☐ 25% to 50%

   4 ☐ More than 50%

   8 ☐ Don't know

21. **What is the zipcode of your practice location where you see most of your TRICARE patients?**

   ZIP CODE: ☐☐☐☐☐   **OR**   8 ☐ Don't Know

22. **In general, for how many of your TRICARE patients do you know where they fill the prescriptions you write?**

   (Check One)

   1 ☐ All

   2 ☐ Most

   3 ☐ Some

   4 ☐ Only a few

   0 ☐ None

8

23. To the best of your knowledge: *(Check One Box on Each Line)*

		YES	NO	DON'T KNOW
a.	Can TRICARE beneficiaries obtain prescriptions at no cost at their local Military Treatment Facility (MTF) as long as the medication is listed in that MTF's formulary?..................................	1 ☐	0 ☐	8 ☐
b.	Do TRICARE beneficiaries pay different co-payments depending on where (e.g. MTF, retail pharmacies, or mail order program) they choose to fill the prescriptions you write?...	1 ☐	0 ☐	8 ☐

24. Please indicate how often the following occur: *(Check One Box on Each Line)*

		NEVER	SELDOM	OCCASIONALLY	OFTEN	VERY OFTEN	DON'T KNOW
a.	Your TRICARE patients complain about certain drugs not being available at their MTF pharmacy.	0 ☐	1 ☐	2 ☐	3 ☐	4 ☐	8 ☐
b.	Your TRICARE patients complain about certain drugs not being available through the TRICARE mail order drug program.	0 ☐	1 ☐	2 ☐	3 ☐	4 ☐	8 ☐
c.	Your TRICARE patients complain to you about their out-of-pocket expenses (e.g. co-payments) for prescriptions.	0 ☐	1 ☐	2 ☐	3 ☐	4 ☐	8 ☐
d.	You advise your TRICARE patients to go to their MTF to have their prescription filled.	0 ☐	1 ☐	2 ☐	3 ☐	4 ☐	8 ☐
e.	Your TRICARE patients ask you to prescribe drugs that they have seen advertised.	0 ☐	1 ☐	2 ☐	3 ☐	4 ☐	8 ☐

25. How satisfied are you that your TRICARE patients can get any drug, when clinically indicated?

(Check One Only)

1 ☐ Very satisfied

2 ☐ Satisfied

3 ☐ Not satisfied

8 ☐ Can't say

This last section inquires about the scope of your practice and your background.

26. **In a typical workweek, how many hours do you spend doing professional activities?** *Your best estimate is fine.*

    # OF HOURS: ☐☐☐

27. **On average, what percentage of your time per week do you spend doing each of the following professional activities?** *Your best estimate is fine.*

    % OF TIME PER WEEK

    a. Management or administration .... ☐☐☐ %

    b. Seeing patients (either by yourself or accompanied by other providers) .... ☐☐☐ %

    c. Didactic teaching (i.e. giving lectures or clinical tutorials) .... ☐☐☐ %

    d. Research .... ☐☐☐ %

    e. Other professional activity .... ☐☐☐ %

       *(please specify):*_____

    TOTAL 100%

28. **In what type of setting do you see (either by yourself or accompanied by other providers) the <u>most</u> patients per week?**
    (Check One Only)

    1 ☐ Clinic-based

    2 ☐ Hospital-based

    3 ☐ Other *(please specify)* _____

29. **What is your profession?**
    (Check One Only)

    1 ☐ Physician → *(Go to Question #30, next page)*

    2 ☐ Nurse Practitioner *(please indicate the specialty area in which you are currently practicing:*
       _____ _____*)* → *(Skip to Question #32, next page)*

    3 ☐ Physician assistant *(please indicate the specialty area in which you are currently practicing:*
       _____ _____*)* → *(Skip to Question #32, next page)*

    4 ☐ Other *(please specify)* _____ → *(Skip to Question #31, next page)*

OMB Control: 0720-0024
Expiration Date: 6/30/2003

30. **If you are a physician, what is your current status?**
(Check One Only)

1 ☐ Completed training (i.e. staff, attending and/or in private practice)

In Training ⟶ 2 ☐ Fellow

3 ☐ Intern

4 ☐ Resident

5 ☐ Other *(please specify)* _____

31. **What is your *primary* area of specialty?**
(Check One Only)

1 ☐ Family Practice/Family Medicine

2 ☐ Geriatrics

3 ☐ General Internal Medicine

4 ☐ Internal Medicine subspecialty *(please specify)* _____

5 ☐ Obstetrics & Gynecology

6 ☐ Pediatrics

7 ☐ Dermatology

8 ☐ Other *(please specify)* _____

32. **How would you characterize the make-up of the outpatient practice where you spend most of your patient care time?**
(Check One Only)

1 ☐ Solo practice (i.e. where you are the only health care provider)

2 ☐ Single-specialty group (i.e. where you practice with other health care providers in your same specialty area)

3 ☐ Multi-specialty group (i.e. where your practice with other health care providers from different specialty areas)

4 ☐ Other *(please specify)* _____

33. **How old were you on your last birthday?**   AGE: ☐☐

OVER ⟶

Do you have any other comments?

_____
_____
_____
_____
_____
_____
_____
_____
_____
_____
_____
_____
_____
_____

Please return your completed survey to RAND in the pre-paid return envelope provided.

Please do <u>not</u> write your name or address anywhere on the questionnaire or the return envelope.

If you have any other questions or if you are missing your return envelope, please call this toll-free number: 1-866-456-1518.

THANK YOU FOR YOUR TIME

DATE

<FIRST NAMES> <LAST NAME>

<ADDRESS 1>

<ADDRESS 2>

<CITY>, <STATE> <ZIP>

Dear <TITLE> <LAST NAME>:

Your assistance is urgently needed! Congress has directed TRICARE Management Activity (TMA) to evaluate the pharmacy benefits program for patients within the Military Health System (MHS). To this end, TMA has asked RAND, an independent non-profit research organization with extensive experience studying health care systems, to conduct a confidential survey of health care providers who treat MHS beneficiaries.

As a health care provider who treats patients covered by MHS through TRICARE, you have been randomly selected to participate in this study. The aim of this survey is to learn more about your experiences prescribing medication to all of your patients in general and to your TRICARE patients in particular. *Your response to this survey will help the Department of Defense (DoD) better understand how to improve the prescription benefits it offers to military personnel and their families.*

Enclosed please find a self-administered questionnaire for you to complete and return in the postage-paid envelope as soon as possible. This should take you approximately 20 minutes. If you have any comments regarding this burden estimate or any other aspect of this collection of information, please contact the Department of Defense, Washington Headquarters Services, Directories for Information Operations and Reports (OMB control: 0720-0024), 1215 Jefferson Davis Highway, Suite 1204, Arlington, VA 22202-4302.

We want to assure you that your participation in this study is *completely voluntary* and that RAND will keep all of your responses *strictly confidential,* except as required by law. While RAND will provide the DoD with a file containing the responses to this questionnaire, RAND will remove, prior to sharing the data with the DoD, all data from the file that would allow for the identification of any specific individual or health care facility. If you have any questions or concerns regarding this study, please call RAND toll-free at 866-456-1518.

I thank you in advance for your participation in this important study.

Sincerely,

Peter A. Glassman, MBBS, MSc
Study Principal Investigator

\<DATE\>

\<TITLE\> \<FIRST NAMES\> \<LAST NAME\>

\<ADDRESS 1\>

\<ADDRESS 2\>

\<CITY\>, \<STATE\> \<ZIP\>

Dear \<TITLE\> \<LAST NAME\>:

Your input is still needed! I am writing to you once again to urge you to take a few minutes to complete the enclosed questionnaire on medication prescribing. You were selected as part of a national sample of health care providers who treat beneficiaries of the Military Health System. **Even if you only see a few patients covered by the Military Health System, your participation is still critical to the success of this research study.**

This is important and timely research. *Your response will enable the Department of Defense's (DoD) TRICARE Management Activity to consider your experience and opinions in managing pharmacy benefits for patients receiving health care coverage through the Military Health System.*

The DoD's TRICARE Management Activity asked RAND, a private non-profit research organization, to administer this survey. I want to assure you that your participation in this study is *completely voluntary* and that RAND will keep all of your responses confidential, except as required by law. The DoD will not have access to any responses that might identify you or your health care facility.

If you have already responded to this request, I thank you for your time. If you have not, we would appreciate if you could please do so as soon as possible. We have included a postage-paid envelope for your convenience. This should take you approximately 20 minutes. If you have any comments regarding this burden estimate or any other aspect of this collection of information, please contact the Department of Defense, Washington Headquarters Services, Directories for Information Operations and Reports (OMB control: 0720-0024), 1215 Jefferson Davis Highway, Suite 1204, Arlington, VA 22202-4302.

Should you have any questions, please feel free to contact Ana Suarez at RAND. She can be reached toll free at 1-866-456-1518.

Thank you.

Sincerely,

Peter A. Glassman, MBBS, MSc
Study Principal Investigator

PLEASE READ

HAVE FORMULARIES AFFECTED YOUR PRESCRIBING PRACTICES?

WHAT DO <u>YOU</u> THINK ARE THE PROS AND CONS OF FORMULARIES?

The Department of Defense Military Health System would like to hear your thoughts on these and other questions regarding formulary systems!

You were randomly selected for this study from among a group of providers who in the past have treated patients covered by TRICARE, the insurance program for military retirees and their families as well as for dependents of active duty military personnel. The Department of Defense (DoD) TRICARE Management Activity, the entity which oversees this insurance program, is considering significant changes to the prescription benefits it offers its beneficiaries. To help inform these changes, Congress has mandated DoD to conduct a survey of providers who treat TRICARE beneficiaries to assess their experiences prescribing medication within a formulary system and their opinions regarding such systems. RAND, a non-profit research organization, is conducting this survey on behalf of DoD.

We have included a postage-paid envelope for your convenience. This should take you approximately 20 minutes. If you have any comments regarding this burden estimate or any other aspect of this collection of information, please contact the Department of Defense, Washington Headquarters Services, Directories for Information Operations and Reports (OMB control: 0720-0024), 1215 Jefferson Davis Highway, Suite 1204, Arlington, VA 22202-4302.

We want to assure you that your participation in this study is *completely voluntary* and that RAND will keep all of your responses confidential, except as required by law. DoD will not have access to any responses that might identify you or your health care facility. If you have any questions or concerns regarding this study, please call RAND toll-free at 866-456-1518.

THANK YOU!

TO: <TITLE> <FNAME> <LNAME>

FROM: Dr. Peter Glassman, Study Principal Investigator

RE: Department of Defense Study on Medication Prescribing and Formulary Systems

I am writing to you one more time in a final plea to ask you to share your experiences with and opinions of the formularies that you deal with in your daily practice.

We understand your time is limited. However, any information you can provide will help RAND in assisting the Department of Defense to determine the rules and procedures governing TRICARE pharmacy benefits.

Your help is urgently needed. **You were randomly selected for this study from among a small group of providers who have submitted claims to TRICARE.** *Even if you do not currently see TRICARE patients, your responses represent other prescribers who treat military dependents in community settings.*

As you know, TRICARE (formerly known as CHAMPUS) is the insurance program for military retirees and their families and for dependents of active duty military personnel. The Department of Defense (DoD) will be making changes to the TRICARE formulary in the near future. RAND is conducting on behalf of DoD a congressionally mandated survey of prescribers to assure that their comments and experiences are taken into consideration.

You may recall that in early October you received, via Federal Express, a questionnaire entitled **Survey on Medication Prescribing and Prescription Drug Benefits**. Completing the survey should take you approximately 20 minutes. If you have any comments regarding this burden estimate or any other aspect of this collection of information, please contact the Department of Defense, Washington Headquarters Services, Directories for Information Operations and Reports (OMB control: 0720-0024), 1215 Jefferson Davis Highway, Suite 1204, Arlington, VA 22202-4302. We want to assure you that your participation in this study is *completely voluntary* and that RAND will keep all of your responses confidential, except as required by law. DoD will not have access to any responses that might identify you or your health care facility.

To request an additional copy of the questionnaire or if you have any questions regarding this study, please call Ana Suarez toll free at 1-866-456-1518. Or you can contact me directly at 310-478-3711 ext. 48337 or by e-mail at peter.glassman@med.va.gov. THANK YOU!

DOD FORMULARY SURVEY

FOLLOW-UP PROMPTING
TELEPHONE SCRIPT FOR TRICARE SAMPLE

IF YOU REACH A RECORDING:

1. **BASED ON THE GREETING, TRY TO VERIFY THAT YOU HAVE REACHED THE FACILITY/OFFICE OF RESPONDENT.**

    1 YES –**TRY AGAIN LATER**
    2 NO – **CODE AS 'PROB'**
    3 NOT SURE – **TRY AGAIN LATER; MAKE NOTE UNDER "COMMENTS"**

IF A PERSON ANSWERS:

2. Hello, my name is _____, and I'm calling from RAND, a research organization in <Santa Monica, California OR Arlington, VA>. I'm trying to reach <RESPONDENT>. Is he/she available?

    IF NEEDED: Have I reached <R's> office?

    1 INFORMANT DOES NOT KNOW R - **VERIFY NUMBER; IF WRONG NUMBER, CODE AS 'WN' AND BRING TO THE ATTENTION OF SUPERVISOR.**
    2 R DOES NOT WORK AT THIS OFFICE/CLINIC ANYMORE - **GO TO #5**
    3 R AT THIS NUMBER BUT R IS NOT AVAILABLE AT THIS TIME – **GO TO #3**
    4 R AT THIS NUMBER AND R IS AVAILABLE - **GO TO #6**

3. **When would be a good time to reach <RESPONDENT>?**
    a.
1 DATE/TIME SPECIFIED – **GO TO #4; INDICATE DATE & TIME GIVEN**
2 NO SPECIFIC TIME – **GO TO #4**

4. **May I leave a message for <RESPONDENT>?**

    IF LEAVING A MESSAGE WITH A PERSON:
    My name is _____ and I'm calling from RAND, a non-profit research organization, regarding a questionnaire we mailed for a study we are conducting on behalf of the Department of Defense. I would appreciate it if <R> could call me back toll free at (866) 456-1518.

IF LEAVING A MESSAGE ON VOICEMAIL:

This message is for <RESPONDENT>. My name is _____, and I'm calling from RAND, a non-profit research organization, regarding a study we are conducting on behalf of the Department of Defense. We recently sent you a questionnaire and I'm calling to find out if you received it. I would appreciate it if you could call me back at your earliest convenience. The toll free number is (866) 456-1518 and again, my name is _____. I will also follow up with you soon if you are unable to return my call. I want to thank you in advance for your participation in this study.

1   LEFT MESSAGE – **CODE AS 'LM-P' OR 'LM-AM'**
2   UNABLE TO LEAVE MESSAGE – **CODE AS 'SCB'**

5.
a.   How long ago did <R> change offices?

Do you have <R's> new phone number and address?

1   DATE OF DEPARTURE GIVEN AND/OR PHONE NUMBER GIVEN – **CODE AS 'PROB' AND INDICATE INFORMATION GIVEN**
2   NOT KNOWN – **CODE AS 'PROB'**

IF RESPONDENT COMES ON LINE:

6.   Hello, my name is _____, and I'm calling from RAND, a non-profit research organization, regarding a study of prescribers we are conducting on behalf of the Department of Defense. We recently sent you a questionnaire asking you about your experiences prescribing medications and I'm calling to find out if you received the questionnaire.

IF NEEDED: The study packet was mailed to you in early July. It included a questionnaire and a cover letter explaining the study.

IF NEEDED: This study is part of an extensive effort by the U.S. Department of Defense to improve the quality of the healthcare being provided to military personnel and their families. However, this study is not designed to evaluate individual health care providers or health facilities. It simply aims at finding out more about how, in general, military health beneficiaries receive their prescriptions from their providers and the provider's experience prescribing medications to them.

Participation is completely voluntary, and RAND will keep all of your responses strictly confidential. Please be assured that RAND will not release any information that can be linked to an individual or a facility. Even though the Department of Defense is sponsoring this survey, RAND is working independently. Therefore, your identity is protected.

The success of the study depends on our obtaining a representative sample of health care providers serving military health beneficiaries, so your participation is extremely important. You were selected at random from a national pool of health care providers who submitted claims to TRICARE for services provided to patients covered by TRICARE. It should only take you about 15 minutes to complete the questionnaire. We hope we can count on your help.

a. RECEIVED QUESTIONNAIRE AND ALREADY RETURNED IT – **CODE AS 'RC'**
b. RECEIVED QUESTIONNAIRE BUT DIDN'T COMPLETE IT YET - **GO TO #7**
c. STUDY NOT APPLICABLE TO R – **GO TO #8**
d. NEEDS REMAIL – **GO TO #9**
e. REFUSAL - **GO TO #10**

IF RESPONDENT RECEIVED QUESTIONNAIRE:

7.   **When might you be able to return the questionnaire?**

IF NEEDED: We would appreciate it if you could complete as soon as possible since we are scheduled to complete data collection in August in order to meet the deadline for reporting the results of the study to Congress.

1 WILL RETURN – ENTER DATE ON CALL RECORD – **CODE AS 'WC' AND GO TO #12**
2 REFUSAL - **GO TO #10**

124

IF R SAYS QUESTIONNAIRE NOT APPLICABLE:

8. **You were selected for this study based on information we received from the TRICARE Management Activity at the Department of Defense, which indicated that you submitted a claim to TRICARE for services provided to a patient covered by TRICARE. If you see any TRICARE patients and if you have prescribing privileges, then you are eligible to participate in this study.**

    a.   IF YES TO SEES TRICARE PATIENTS <u>AND</u> HAS PRESCRIBING PRIVILEGES – **GO BACK TO OUTCOMES IN #6 AND FOLLOW SCRIPT FOR OUTCOMES #2, #4 OR #5, ACCORDINGLY**

    b.   IF DOESN'T PRESCRIBE MEDICATIONS OR DOESN'T TREAT ANY TRICARE PATIENTS –
    I will make a note of this on our records so that we do not send you any more surveys.
    CODE AS 'NE'

REMAIL:

9. I can re-send the study packet to you. Let me confirm your mailing address.

a. ADDRESS ON FILE VERIFIED - **CODE AS 'RM' AND GO TO # 12**
b. CHANGES TO ADDRESS ON FILE – **CODE AS 'RM' AND GO TO #12; INDICATE CHANGES TO ADDRESS ON CALL RECORD**

REFUSAL:

10. Your participation is critical in order for the results of this study to be as representative as possible of all prescribers who treat military health beneficiaries. We expect the results to be very useful to health care providers, administrators and policymakers within the Military Health System. It should only take you about 15 minutes to complete the survey. I can assure you, we will not share any identifiable information about individuals or their facilities.

    a.   STILL REFUSES – **GO TO #11**
    b.   OBJECTIONS OVERCOME – NEEDS ANOTHER COPY OF SURVEY – **GO TO #9**
    c.   OBJECTIONS OVERCOME – HAS SURVEY – **CODE AS 'WC' AND GO TO #12**

11.   **I am sorry that you do not wish to participate in this study. May I ask why?**

        IF NEEDED: Knowing why a prescriber can not or does not wish to
                       participate in this study will help us better understand if,
                       and how, those who do not participate differ from those
                       who do.

        CODE AS 'R-NI' AND INDICATE REASON GIVEN IF ANY

        IF RESPONDENT SAYS HE/SHE WILL COMPLETE QUESTIONNAIRE:

12.   We really appreciate you taking the time to participate in this survey. *We
        would appreciate it if you complete it and return it as soon as possible since we
        are scheduled to complete data collection in August in order to meet the deadline
        for reporting the results of the study to Congress.* The study packet includes
        a self-addressed and stamped envelope for you to return the
        questionnaire. There is no need for you to write your name or address
        anywhere on the questionnaire. Please be assured that RAND will keep
        all of your responses strictly confidential and that RAND will not make
        your responses public in any way that can be linked to you directly or
        your facility.

        Thank you very much.

        (CODE OUTCOME AND NOTES ON CALL RECORD)

C. Coefficients and Odds Ratios Used in the Non-Response Analysis

The two tables in this appendix provide the inomial logit coefficients and odds ratios calculated for the analysis of non-response discussed in Chapter 4.

Table C.1

Binomial Logit Coefficients and Odds Ratios Predicting Response to Survey of Direct-Care Prescribers

	Logit Coefficient	Odds Ratio
Visit count	−0.000	1.000
	(0.32)	(0.32)
Obstetrician/gynecologist	0.300	1.350
	(0.82)	(0.82)
Subspecialist	0.304	1.355
	(1.16)	(1.16)
Pediatrician	−0.442	0.643
	(1.62)	(1.62)
Non-physician prescriber	0.919	2.507
	(2.18)[a]	(2.18)[a]
Small MTF	0.304	1.355
	(1.08)	(1.08)
Medium MTF	0.109	1.115
	(0.46)	(0.46)
Female	0.399	1.490
	(1.88)[b]	(1.88)[b]
Constant	0.495	—
	(1.77)[b]	—
Number of observations	548	548

NOTE: The absolute value of the z statistic is shown in parentheses. The reference group is the non-respondents. These analyses are not adjusted with the sampling weights because we are not making inferences from our sample to the population of MHS prescribers.

[a]Significant at 5 percent.

[b]Significant at 10 percent.

128

Table C.2

Binomial Logit Coefficients and Odds Ratios Predicting Response to Survey of Purchased-Care Prescribers

	Logit Coefficient	Odds Ratio
Obstetrician/gynecologist	0.680	1.974
	(1.87)[b]	(1.87)[b]
Subspecialist	−0.283	0.753
	(1.14)	(1.14)
Pediatrician	0.331	1.392
	(1.27)	(1.27)
Practice inside MTF catchment area	−0.466	0.627
	(1.97)[a]	(1.97)[a]
Practice partially inside MTF catchment area	−0.021	0.979
	(0.07)	(0.07)
Humana	0.334	1.397
	(0.97)	(0.97)
Triwest	0.383	1.467
	(0.96)	(0.96)
Healthnet	−0.462	0.630
	(1.08)	(1.08)
Number of claims	0.007	1.007
	(1.61)	(1.61)
Amount paid by TRICARE	0.000	1.000
	(0.32)	(0.32)
Constant	−0.819	—
	(2.27)[a]	—
Number of observations	468	468

NOTE: The absolute value of the z statistic is shown in parentheses. The reference group is the non-respondents. These analyses are not adjusted with the sampling weights because we are not making inferences from our sample to the population of MHS prescribers.

[a]Significant at 5 percent.

[b]Significant at 10 percent.

D. Detailed Data on Survey Responses

In this appendix, we present several tables displaying data on the survey responses from both the direct-care and purchased-care respondents. The tables are organized according to sections of the survey instruments. For the direct-care survey, results are presented by specialty type and MTF size. For the purchased-care survey, results are presented by specialty type and TRICARE patient load. Survey responses are presented by survey topic area. As described in Chapter 5, we performed two types of statistical tests. The table notes indicate where statistical differences were observed.

Table D.1

Feedback on Prescribing Experiences over the Past Three Months

| | Direct-Care System | | | | | | | Purchased-Care System | | | | |
| | | MTF Size | | | Specialty | | | | Caseload | | Specialty | |
	Total	Small	Medium	Large	Primary	Secondary	PA/APN	Total	Light	Heavy	Primary	Secondary
N	375	105	119	151	206	111	59	155	88	62	87	63

In the past 3 months how often have you:

Changed medication because it was not available in formulary? (percentage of respondents)[g]

	Total	Small	Medium	Large	Primary	Secondary	PA/APN	Total	Light	Heavy	Primary	Secondary
Never	19	10	21	22	16	25[a,h]	18	2	3	6	0	4
1–5 times	55	63	57	52	55	54[a,h]	50	26	29	36	23	26
6–10 times	15	14	10	18	15	13[a,h]	22	27	31	23	33	16
11–20 times	8	10	8	8	10	6[a,h]	8	27	20	25	32	22
>20 times	2	3	5	1	4	1[a,h]	2	18	17	11	12	32

Not prescribed a non-formulary medication because you thought the request would be denied? (percentage of respondents)[g]

	Total	Small	Medium	Large	Primary	Secondary	PA/APN	Total	Light	Heavy	Primary	Secondary
Never	60	57	62	60	58	63[a,h]	53	13	26	14	7	16
1–5 times	33	33	31	33	32	32[a,h]	37	36	35	38	43	29
6–10 times	4	7	5	3	5	4[a,h]	3	20	17	18	18	16
11–20 times	2	2	0	3	3	1[a,h]	3	14	8	20	16	15
>20 times	1	1	2	1	2	1[a,h]	3	16	14	9	16	24

Table D.1—Continued

| | Direct-Care System | | | | | | | Purchased-Care System | | | | |
| | MTF Size | | | | Specialty | | | Caseload | | | Specialty | |
	Total	Small	Medium	Large	Primary	Secondary	PA/APN	Total	Light	Heavy	Primary	Secondary
In the past 3 months how often have you:												
Not prescribed a non-formulary medication because you thought the request would take too long? (percentage of respondents)[g]												
Never	52	49	55	53	52	56	51	42	47	42	31	41
1–5 times	32	33	31	32	32	31	32	28	25	31	42	13
6–10 times	10	11	8	10	8	9	11	11	16	12	8	24
11–20 times	3	5	4	2	4	2	3	9	3	9	8	9
>20 times	3	3	1	4	4	1	3	9	10	5	11	12
Advised patients to obtain a non-formulary drug outside MTF? (percentage of respondents)[g]												
Never	34	33	32	35	28	44[a,h]	34[e,h]	N/A	N/A	N/A	N/A	N/A
1–5 times	48	46	53	47	48	45[a,h]	45[e,h]	N/A	N/A	N/A	N/A	N/A
6–10 times	10	14	12	8	14	6[a,h]	12[e,h]	N/A	N/A	N/A	N/A	N/A
11–20 times	4	6	1	5	6	3[a,h]	5[e,h]	N/A	N/A	N/A	N/A	N/A
>20 times	4	2	1	5	4	2[a,h]	4[e,h]	N/A	N/A	N/A	N/A	N/A

Table D.1—Continued

	Direct-Care System — MTF Size: Total	Small	Medium	Large	Direct-Care Specialty: Primary	Secondary	PA/APN	Purchased-Care Caseload: Total	Light	Heavy	Purchased Specialty: Primary	Secondary
Never	52	49	55	53	52	56	51	42	47	42	31	41
1–5 times	32	33	31	32	32	31	32	28	25	31	42	13
6–10 times	10	11	8	10	8	9	11	11	16	12	8	24
11–20 times	3	5	4	2	4	2	3	9	3	9	8	9
>20 times	3	3	1	4	4	1	3	9	10	5	11	12

Advised patients to obtain a non-formulary drug outside MTF? (percentage of respondents)[g]

	Total	Small	Medium	Large	Primary	Secondary	PA/APN	Total	Light	Heavy	Primary	Secondary
Never	34	33	32	35	28	44[a,h]	34[e,h]	N/A	N/A	N/A	N/A	N/A
1–5 times	48	46	53	47	48	45[a,h]	45[e,h]	N/A	N/A	N/A	N/A	N/A
6–10 times	10	14	12	8	14	6[a,h]	12[e,h]	N/A	N/A	N/A	N/A	N/A
11–20 times	4	6	1	5	6	3[a,h]	5[e,h]	N/A	N/A	N/A	N/A	N/A
>20 times	4	2	1	5	4	2[a,h]	4[e,h]	N/A	N/A	N/A	N/A	N/A

Table D.1—Continued

	Direct-Care System							Purchased-Care System				
		MTF Size			Specialty				Caseload		Specialty	
	Total	Small	Medium	Large	Primary	Secondary	PA/APN	Total	Light	Heavy	Primary	Secondary
In the past 3 months how often have you:												
Been asked by a patient to prescribe a non-formulary drug, even though a formulary drug is just as effective? (percentage of respondents)g												
Never	33	39	33	31	33	39	26e,h	43	48	50	37	43
1–5 times	52	47	53	53	49	51	50e,h	41	37	38	38	43
6–10 times	13	12	11	13	14	9	18e,h	11	10	7	20	4
11–20 times	1	0	2	1	1	1	2e,h	5	2	6	5	9
> 20 times	2	2	1	2	2	1	4e,h	1	3	0	1	1
Requested approval for a non-formulary drug because the patient requested it? (percentage of respondents)												
Never	N/A							71	68	81	59	64
1–5 times	N/A							22	22	16	29	26
6–10 times	N/A							5	6	3	7	6
11–20 times	N/A							0	0	0	0	0
> 20 times	N/A							3	3	0	5	4

aDirect Care: Significant difference from small MTF or from primary care at 0.05 level.
bDirect Care: Significant difference from small MTF or from primary care at 0.01 level.
cPurchased Care: Significant difference at 0.05 level.
dPurchased Care: Significant difference at 0.01 level.
eDirect Care: Significant difference from medium-sized MTF or secondary provider at 0.05 level.
fDirect Care: Significant difference from medium-sized MTF or secondary provider at 0.01 level.
gExcludes "don't know" responses.
hTest of equivalence of distribution of responses.
iDirect Care: Respondents who indicated ever making a request for a non-formulary medication.
jPurchased Care: Respondents who were familiar with formularies.
N/A = Not applicable

Table D.2

Attitudes About and Impact of Formularies and Preferred Lists

| | Total | Direct-Care System | | | | | | Purchased-Care System | | | | |
| | | MTF Size | | | Specialty | | | Total | Caseload | | Specialty | |
		Small	Medium	Large	Primary	Secondary	PA/APN		Light	Heavy	Primary	Secondary
N	382	108	122	152	211	112	59	162	99	64	88	66

Formularies/lists help my ability to prescribe clinically appropriate drugs. (% of respondents)

	Total	Small	Medium	Large	Primary	Secondary	PA/APN	Total	Light	Heavy	Primary	Secondary
Agree	64	60	66	64	65	57	69	9	8	9	10	7
Neutral	26	27	25	26	26	28	20	11	13	14	15	25
Disagree	11	13	9	10	9	15	11	80	78	77	75	71

My patients can obtain non-formulary/preferred drugs when medically justified. (% of respondents)

	Total	Small	Medium	Large	Primary	Secondary	PA/APN	Total	Light	Heavy	Primary	Secondary
Agree	93	88	86	97[b,f,h]	92	95	85[e,h]	45	46	48	38	47
Neutral	5	10	11	2[b,f,h]	7	3	8[e,h]	32	28	28	34	18
Disagree	2	2	2	1[b,f,h]	1	1	7[e,h]	23	26	24	27	35

[a] Direct Care: Significant difference from small MTF or from primary care at 0.05 level.

[b] Direct Care: Significant difference from small MTF or from primary care at 0.01 level.

[c] Purchased Care: Significant difference at 0.05 level.

[d] Purchased Care: Significant difference at 0.01 level.

[e] Direct Care: Significant difference from medium-sized MTF or secondary provider at 0.05 level.

[f] Direct Care: Significant difference from medium-sized MTF or secondary provider at 0.01 level.

[g] Excludes "don't know" responses.

[h] Test of equivalence of distribution of responses.

[i] Direct Care: Respondents who indicated ever making a request for a non-formulary medication.

[j] Purchased Care: Respondents who were familiar with formularies.

Table D.3

Opinions About Easing Compliance with Formularies

	Direct-Care System							Purchased-Care System				
	MTF Size				Primary	Specialty		Total	Caseload		Specialty	
	Total	Small	Medium	Large		Secondary	PA/APN		Light	Heavy	Primary	Secondary
N	376	104	120	152	207	111	58	162	91	64	88	66
What would make it easier to comply with formulary lists? (check all that apply) (% of respondents)												
Feedback on prescription patterns	42	44	48	40	47	36	40	12	16	16	7 [c]	19
Regular reminders on content	48	48	45	48	49	36[a]	62[f]	27	31	21	21	35
Electronic prescribing	49	42	50	53	43	60[b]	36[f]	18	18	20	22	17
Regularly updated lists	54	62	47 [a]	54	56	46	59	44	12	11	42	53
Web-based lists	36	37	37	37	34	40	32	12	25	30	12	6

Table D.3—Continued

	Direct-Care System							Purchased-Care System				
	Total	MTF Size			Specialty		PA/APN	Total	Caseload		Specialty	
		Small	Medium	Large	Primary	Secondary			Light	Heavy	Primary	Secondary
What would make it easier to comply with formulary lists? (check all that apply) (% of respondents)												
Better responsiveness to providers' concerns	32	38	33	30	31	34	36	23	24	14	21	18

[a] Direct Care: Significant difference from small MTF or from primary care at 0.05 level.
[b] Direct Care: Significant difference from small MTF or from primary care at 0.01 level.
[c] Purchased Care: Significant difference at 0.05 level.
[d] Purchased Care: Significant difference at 0.01 level.
[e] Direct Care: Significant difference from medium-sized MTF or secondary provider at 0.05 level.
[f] Direct Care: Significant difference from medium-sized MTF or secondary provider at 0.01 level.
[g] Excludes "don't know" responses.
[h] Test of equivalence of distribution of responses.
[i] Direct Care: Respondents who indicated ever making a request for a non-formulary medication.
[j] Purchased Care: Respondents who were familiar with formularies.

Table D.4

Opinions on Overall Pharmacy Management

| | Direct-Care System | | | | | | | Purchased-Care System | | | | |
| | | MTF Size | | | Specialty | | | | Caseload | | Specialty | |
	Total	Small	Medium	Large	Primary	Secondary	PA/APN	Total	Light	Heavy	Primary	Secondary
N	382	108	122	152	211	112	59	162	91	63	87	66

It is easy to keep track of changes to formularies/lists. (% of respondents)

	Total	Small	Medium	Large	Primary	Secondary	PA/APN	Total	Light	Heavy	Primary	Secondary
Agree	47	46	53	45	51	43	41	10	10	5	9	6
Neutral	16	19	18	14	14	21	20	3	8	3	8	6
Disagree	38	35	29	41	35	36	38	87	82	92	83	88

Formularies/lists have done a good job of keeping drugs up-to-date in the drug classes I would like to prescribe. (% of respondents)

	Total	Small	Medium	Large	Primary	Secondary	PA/APN	Total	Light	Heavy	Primary	Secondary
Agree	67	61	72	68	71	55[a,h]	69	15	20	5	13	15
Neutral	19	16	13	23	16	25[a,h]	14	27	32	42	36	21
Disagree	14	23	15	10	13	20[a,h]	18	58	48	53	51	63

It is important for health plans/MTFs to save money by choosing for their lists the best drug with the best value within its therapeutic class. (% of respondents)

	Total	Small	Medium	Large	Primary	Secondary	PA/APN	Total	Light	Heavy	Primary	Secondary
Agree	87	82	88[a,h]	87	88	87	76[a,h]	40	48	42	42	50
Neutral	9	12	8[a,h]	8	9	6	13[a,h]	33	24	29	26	25
Disagree	5	6	4[a,h]	4	3	7	11[a,h]	28	28	29	32	25

Table D.4—Continued

	Direct-Care System							Purchased-Care System				
	MTF Size				Specialty		PA/APN	Total	Caseload		Specialty	
	Total	Small	Medium	Large	Primary	Secondary			Light	Heavy	Primary	Secondary
The drug restrictions imposed by formularies/lists are necessary for containing costs in a health plan. (% of respondents)												
Agree	80	71	80	83[a,h]	80	80	74	33	34	42	34	49
Neutral	14	19	11	12[a,h]	13	15	9	39	38	42	39	18
Disagree	6	10	9	4[a,h]	7	5	17	29	28	16	28	33
Overall, I am satisfied with the non-formulary waiver/approval process in my MTF. (% of respondents)												
Agree	78	71	76	82	76	82	68[e,h]			N/A		
Neutral	13	23	14	9	15	13	18[e,h]			N/A		
Disagree	9	6	11	9	10	4	14[e,h]			N/A		

[a]Direct Care: Significant difference from small MTF or from primary care at 0.05 level.
[b]Direct Care: Significant difference from small MTF or from primary care at 0.01 level.
[c]Purchased Care: Significant difference at 0.05 level.
[d]Purchased Care: Significant difference at 0.01 level.
[e]Direct Care: Significant difference from medium-sized MTF or secondary provider at 0.05 level.
[f]Direct Care: Significant difference from medium-sized MTF or secondary provider at 0.01 level.
[g]Excludes "don't know" responses.
[h]Test of equivalence of distribution of responses.
[i]Direct Care: Respondents who indicated ever making a request for a non-formulary medication.
[j]Purchased Care: Respondents who were familiar with formularies.

Table D.5

Feedback on Role and Effectiveness of P&T Committees

	Direct-Care System							Purchased-Care System				
	MTF Size				Specialty		PA/APN	Total	Caseload		Specialty	
	Total	Small	Medium	Large	Primary	Secondary			Light	Heavy	Primary	Secondary
Degree of familiarity with activities of P&T committee (% of respondents)												
N	381	108	122	151	211	112	58					
Very Familiar	30	30	38	27 e, h	33	27	26		Not assessed		Not assessed	Not assessed
Somewhat familiar	49	45	47	51 e, h	45	55	51					
Not at all familiar	21	25	15	22 e, h	22	18	23					
P&T committees are responsive to the concerns of providers. (% of respondents)												
N	305	82	104	119	169	91	45	162	91	63	87	66
Agree	84	83	83	86	85	79	87	34	30	22	26	21
Neutral	11	8	8	13	10	15	9	39	40	43	37	35
Disagree	5	9	9	1	5	6	4	29	30	35	37	44
I have confidence in the ability of P&T committees to choose the safest and most clinically effective drugs. (% of respondents)												
N	305	82	104	119	169	91	45	162	91	63	87	66
Agree	83	80	83	83 e, h	84	79	87	23	22	17	21	23
Neutral	11	11	11	13 e, h	10	15	9	33	34	44	37	36
Disagree	6	9	7	4 e, h	6	6	4	44	44	39	4	31

Table D.5—Continued

| | Direct-Care System | | | | | | | Purchased-Care System | | | | |
| | MTF Size | | | | Specialty | | | | Caseload | | Specialty | |
	Total	Small	Medium	Large	Primary	Secondary	PA/APN	Total	Light	Heavy	Primary	Secondary
I have confidence in the ability of P&T committees to choose the drugs with the best value. (% of respondents)												
N	305	82	104	119	169	91	45	162	91	63	87	66
Agree	88	87	85	90	88	87	93	20	36	46	39	42
Neutral	9	11	9	9	11	11	0	37	40	32	36	38
Disagree	3	2	6	1	1	2	7	43	24	22	26	20
Overall, I am satisfied with the decisions and actions of the P&T committee. (% of respondents)												
N	305	82	104	119	169	91	45					
Agree	84	82	82	87	85	82	86			Not assessed		
Neutral	11	8	8	12	10	12	12			Not assessed		
Disagree	5	10	9	1	4	6	2			Not assessed		

[a]Direct Care: Significant difference from small MTF or from primary care at 0.05 level.
[b]Direct Care: Significant difference from small MTF or from primary care at 0.01 level.
[c]Purchased Care: Significant difference at 0.05 level.
[d]Purchased Care: Significant difference at 0.01 level.
[e]Direct Care: Significant difference from medium-sized MTF or secondary provider at 0.05 level.
[f]Direct Care: Significant difference from medium-sized MTF or secondary provider at 0.01 level.
[g]Excludes "don't know" responses.
[h]Test of equivalence of distribution of responses.
[i]Direct Care: Respondents who indicated ever making a request for a non-formulary medication.
[j]Purchased Care: Respondents who were familiar with formularies.

Table D.6

Feedback on Burden of Outside Prescriptions on MTF, Direct-Care Prescribers Only

| | | Direct-Care System | | | | | |
| | | MTF Size | | | Specialty | | |
	Total	Small	Medium	Large	Primary	Secondary	PA/APN
Patients filling prescriptions written by outside providers drain MTF resources. (% of respondents)							
N	382	108	122	152	211	112	59
Agree	39	31	50[b,h]	39[a,h]	42	34	37
Neutral	35	31	28[b,h]	38[a,h]	32	43	28
Disagree	26	38	22[b,h]	23[a,h]	26	23	36
Rewriting outside prescriptions is burdensome to prescribers at MTFs. (% of respondents)							
N	382	108	122	152	211	112	59
Agree	58	48	68[b,h]	58	62	51	58
Neutral	28	28	21[b,h]	30	23	34	23
Disagree	14	23	11[b,h]	12	15	15	19
Number of times you have been asked by a patient to re-write a prescription from a non-MTF provider to be filled at MTF (% of respondents)[g]							
N	378	106	121	151	207	112	59
Never	46	49	56	42[e,h]	44	55	43
1–5 times	42	44	35	43[e,h]	44	38	40
6–10 times	9	5	6	11[e,h]	8	6	12
11–20 times	3	2	2	3[e,h]	4	0	5
> 20 times	1	1	1	1[e,h]	1	2	0

Table D.6—Continued

	Direct-Care System						
	MTF Size				Specialty		
	Total	Small	Medium	Large	Primary	Secondary	PA/APN
Number of times you have requested a non-formulary drug originally prescribed outside MTF because patient wanted to fill prescription at the MTF (% of respondents)[i]							
Never	63	49	60	68[a,h]	53	71	54
1–5 times	33	47	36	28[a,h]	42	23	41
6–10 times	2	3	3	2[a,h]	2	4	0
11–20 times	1	0	0	2[a,h]	1	0	3
>20 times	0	0	1	0[a,h]	0	0	3
For hypothetical new MTF patient taking non-formulary drug, what would you do first? (% of respondents)[g]							
N	377	107	120	150	207	112	58
Convert patient to similar formulary drug	86	85	88	86	83	88	84
Request approval for non-formulary drug	11	10	12	12	13	12	9
Advise patient to obtain drug outside MTF	3	5	0	2	4	0	7

[a]Direct Care: Significant difference from small MTF or from primary care at 0.05 level.

[b]Direct Care: Significant difference from small MTF or from primary care at 0.01 level.

[c]Purchased Care: Significant difference at 0.05 level.

[d]Purchased Care: Significant difference at 0.01 level.

[e]Direct Care: Significant difference from medium-sized MTF or secondary provider at 0.05 level.

[f]Direct Care: Significant difference from medium-sized MTF or secondary provider at 0.01 level.

[g]Excludes "don't know" responses.

[h]Test of equivalence of distribution of responses.

[i]Direct Care: Respondents who indicated ever making a request for a non-formulary medication.

[j]Purchased Care: Respondents who were familiar with formularies.

Table D.7

Feedback on Experiences Obtaining Approval for Non-Formulary and Non-Preferred Drugs

	Direct-Care System							Purchased-Care System				
		MTF Size			Specialty				Caseload		Specialty	
	Total	Small	Medium	Large	Primary	Secondary	PA/APN	Total	Light	Heavy	Primary	Secondary
Requested approval for non-formulary/non-preferred drug (% of respondents)[j]												
N	379	107	121	151	208	112	59	160	93	65	90	66
Yes	88	84	89	89	89	92	76[a,e]	84	82	79	86	75
How long does it generally take to find out if a non-formulary drug is approved? (% of respondents)[g, i]												
N	292	82	91	117	163	90	39	Not assessed				
<1 day	26	26	26	27	29	28	18	Not assessed				
1–2 days	27	35	23	26	26	29	31	Not assessed				
3–5 days	20	15	30	18	20	23	14	Not assessed				
> 5 days	27	24	21	29	25	19	36	Not assessed				
Mean number of requests for non-formulary/non-preferred drugs in the past three months (% of respondents)[i, j]												
N	314	86	101	127	170	102	42	114	63	49	64	47
Mean	7.2	6.7	9.4	6.6[e]	6.5	9.1[a]	5.0[f]	10.4	10.1	9.0	8.4	15.6
Standard deviation	(8.2)	(7.9)	(13.0)	(5.9)	(7.8)	(9.2)	(5.4)	(16.9)	(19.7)	(14.6)	(8.2)	(25.4)
Mean number of requests denied in past three months for those requesting in past three months (% of respondents)												
N	271	86	94	112	149	90	32	99	53	44	59	37
Mean	0.3	6.7	0.5	0.3	0.3	0.3	1	2.8	3.3	2.2	2.3	4.5
Standard deviation	(0.9)	(7.9)	(1.5)	(0.8)	(0.8)	(0.8)	(2.4)	(9.8)	(12.9)	(2.9)	(3.5)	(10.3)

143

Table D.7—Continued

| | Direct-Care System | | | | | | | Purchased-Care System | | | | |
| | | MTF Size | | | Specialty | | | | Caseload | | Specialty | |
	Total	Small	Medium	Large	Primary	Secondary	PA/APN	Total	Light	Heavy	Primary	Secondary
Actions taken upon denial for those who made requests and received denial in the past three months (check all that apply) (% of respondents)j												
N	72	20	23	29	36	21	15	62	30	31	35	26
Appeal denial	13	9	40[a]	6[e]	10	16	8	24	28	24	19	23
Resubmitted request w/ more info.	25	22	15	29	27	30	24	55	35	47	45	52
Sought approval for different non-formulary drug	1	0	5	0	0	0	4	9	16	7	20	8
Prescribed formulary drug	18	11	11	23	14	16	24	49	41	44	65	50
Advised obtaining non-formulary drug outside MTF	39	46	39	36	34	39	43	N/A				

Table D.7—Continued

| | Direct-Care System | | | | | | | Purchased-Care System | | | | |
| | MTF Size | | | | Specialty | | | | Caseload | | Specialty | |
	Total	Small	Medium	Large	Primary	Secondary	PA/APN	Total	Light	Heavy	Primary	Secondary
Impact of non-formulary denial on patient health for those who made request and received denial in past three months (% of respondents)[g,j]												
N	49	10	18	21	24	14	11	51	24	27	30	20
Too soon to tell	26	5	51	22	29	37	6	31	18	25	28[d,h]	18
Unaffected	57	78	32	62	53	53	71	24	51	37	62[d,h]	16
Minor decline	1	18	0	14	18	0	12	43	28	34	10[d,h]	57
Major decline	5	0	17	2	0	10	12	2	3	5	0[d,h]	10

[a]Direct Care: Significant difference from small MTF or from primary care at 0.05 level.
[b]Direct Care: Significant difference from small MTF or from primary care at 0.01 level.
[c]Purchased Care: Significant difference at 0.05 level.
[d]Purchased Care: Significant difference at 0.01 level.
[e]Direct Care: Significant difference from medium-sized MTF or secondary provider at 0.05 level.
[f]Direct Care: Significant difference from medium-sized MTF or secondary provider at 0.01 level.
[g]Excludes "don't know" responses.
[h]Test of equivalence of distribution of responses.
[i]Direct Care: Respondents who indicated ever making a request for a non-formulary medication.
[j]Purchased Care: Respondents who were familiar with formularies.

Table D.8

Feedback on Patients' Complaints About Out-of-Pocket Costs

| | Direct-Care System | | | | | | | Purchased-Care System | | | | |
| | | MTF Size | | | Specialty | | | | Caseload | | Specialty | |
	Total	Small	Medium	Large	Primary	Secondary	PA/APN	Total	Light	Heavy	Primary	Secondary
How often do you hear complaints from patients about out-of-pocket expenses for their prescriptions? (% of respondents)g												
N	377	106	121	150	207	112	58	181	102	78	96	79
Never	49	42	49	56	48	57	36e, h	71	24	19	19	18
Seldom	37	45	36	34	43	28	44e, h	43	43	41	46	46
Occasionally	12	12	13	10	10	13	18e, h	26	19	34	22	26
Often	1	1	0	1	1	1	2e, h	7	11	6	12	7
Very often	1	0	3	0	0	1	0e, h	2	3	0	2	3

aDirect Care: Significant difference from small MTF or from primary care at 0.05 level.

bDirect Care: Significant difference from small MTF or from primary care at 0.01 level.

cPurchased Care: Significant difference at 0.05 level.

dPurchased Care: Significant difference at 0.01 level.

eDirect Care: Significant difference from medium-sized MTF or secondary provider at 0.05 level.

fDirect Care: Significant difference from medium-sized MTF or secondary provider at 0.01 level.

gExcludes "don't know" responses.

hTest of equivalence of distribution of responses.

iDirect Care: Respondents who indicated ever making a request for a non-formulary medication.

jPurchased Care: Respondents who were familiar with formularies.

Table D.9

Feedback on the Effects of a Tiered Co-Payment System, Purchased-Care Prescribers Only

| | Total | Caseload | | Specialty | |
		Light	Heavy	Primary	Secondary
N	214	131	78	114	95
A tiered co-payment system promotes cost-effective prescribing. (% of respondents)					
Agree	44	54	40	44	56
Neutral	33	28	41	26	23
Disagree	23	19	19	30	22
A tiered co-payment system places an unfair burden on patients. (% of respondents)					
Agree	36	37	34	36	44
Neutral	36	32	38	35	28
Disagree	28	31	28	22	22
A tiered co-payment system limits the effect of drug advertising. (% of respondents)					
Agree	33	38	26	34	33
Neutral	48	43	46	44	46
Disagree	19	19	29	23	22

Table D.10

Feedback on Impact of Direct-to-Consumer Marketing

| | Direct-Care System | | | | | | | Purchased-Care System | | | | |
| | | MTF Size | | | Specialty | | | | Caseload | | Specialty | |
	Total	Small	Medium	Large	Primary	Secondary	PA/APN	Total	Light	Heavy	Primary	Secondary
Number of times you have been asked by a patient to prescribe a drug because patient had seen it advertised (% of respondents) [g]												
N	378	106	120	152	207	112	59	189	110	77	100	83
Never	23	29	24	21	26	28	8 [b,f,h]	9	19 [c,h]	6	6	16
1–5 times	39	41	47	35	39	44	43 [b,f,h]	49	51 [c,h]	47	48	42
6–10 times	25	15	18	31	21	23	26 [b,f,h]	33	28 [c,h]	38	30	34
11–20 times	8	12	6	7	10	2	9 [b,f,h]	4	1 [c,h]	5	9	5
>20 times	5	3	5	6	4	4	14 [b,f,h]	4	1 [c,h]	4	6	3
How often do TRICARE patients ask for drugs they have seen advertised? (% of respondents) [g]												
N	N/A							168	99	65	94	70
Never	N/A							15	22	17	14	13
Seldom	N/A							53	51	50	43	54
Occasionally	N/A							19	17	21	25	18
Often	N/A							3	5	3	6	9
Very Often	N/A							9	5	9	12	6

Table D.10—Continued

| | Direct-Care System | | | | | | | Purchased-Care System | | | | |
| | Total | MTF Size | | | Specialty | | | Total | Caseload | | Specialty | |
		Small	Medium	Large	Primary	Secondary	PA/APN		Light	Heavy	Primary	Secondary
Direct-to-consumer advertising prompts patients to seek care for health conditions that might otherwise go untreated. (% of respondents)												
N	382	108	122	152	211	112	59	215	132	79	114	95
Agree	48	46	45	50	44	54	47	47	43	47	36 [d,h]	59
Neutral	32	30	35	32	33	30	39	23	21	26	28 [d,h]	16
Disagree	20	24	20	18	23	16	14	30	36	27	36 [d,h]	26
Patients' requests for advertised drugs make my job more challenging. (% of respondents)												
N	382	108	122	152	211	112	59	215	132	79	114	95
Agree	56	47	57	59	55	54	65	46	46	49	50	43
Neutral	22	29	23	19	21	27	15	29	31	24	27	32
Disagree	22	23	20	22	24	19	20	24	23	28	23	25

[a]Direct Care: Significant difference from small MTF or from primary care at 0.05 level.

[b]Direct Care: Significant differences from small MTF or from primary care at 0.01 level.

[c]Purchased Care: Significant difference at 0.05 level.

[d]Purchased Care: Significant difference at 0.01 level.

[e]Direct Care: Significant difference from medium-sized MTF or secondary provider at 0.05 level.

[f]Direct Care: Significant difference from medium-sized MTF or secondary provider at 0.01 level.

[g]Excludes "don't know" responses.

[h]Test of equivalence of distribution of responses.

[i]Direct Care: Respondents who indicated ever making a request for a non-formulary medication.

[j]Purchased Care: Respondents who were familiar with formularies.

Table D.11

Perceptions of TRICARE Patients' Access to Pharmaceuticals, Purchased-Care System Prescribers Only

| | | Purchased-Care System | | | |
| | | Caseload | | Specialty | |
	Total	Light	Heavy	Primary	Secondary
How often do the following occur?					
TRICARE patients complain about drugs not being available at MTF pharmacy. (% of respondents)g					
N	181	100	78	96	79
Never	3	13	2	5	1
Seldom	17	13	20	12	15
Occasionally	44	47	41	42	53
Often	18	19	25	26	20
Very Often	15	9	11	15	11
TRICARE patients complain about drugs not being available through TRICARE mail order drug program. (% of respondents)g					
N	142	78	62	76	61
Never	22	29	20	23	18
Seldom	30	28	28	26	30
Occasionally	37	33	42	36	43
Often	6	12	6	9	5
Very Often	6	2	5	5	4

Table D.11—Continued

		Purchased-Care System			
		Caseload		Specialty	
	Total	Light	Heavy	Primary	Secondary
How often does the following occur?					
You advise TRICARE patients to go to their MTF to get prescription filled. (% of respondents)					
N	185	107	77	98	82
Never	27	57[c, h]	26	29[c, h]	13
Seldom	6	1[c, h]	3	10[c, h]	8
Occasionally	19	16[c, h]	18	17[c, h]	19
Often	24	18[c, h]	20	19[c, h]	37
Very Often	24	8[c, h]	32	23[c, h]	23

[a]Direct Care: Significant difference from small MTF or from primary care at 0.05 level.
[b]Direct Care: Significant difference from small MTF or from primary care at 0.01 level.
[c]Purchased Care: Significant difference at 0.05 level.
[d]Purchased Care: Significant difference at 0.01 level.
[e]Direct Care: Significant difference from medium-sized MTF or secondary provider at 0.05 level.
[f]Direct Care: Significant difference from medium-sized MTF or secondary provider at 0.01 level.
[g]Excludes "don't know" responses.
[h]Test of equivalence of distribution of responses.
[i]Direct Care: Respondents who indicated ever making a request for a non-formulary medication.
[j]Purchased Care: Respondents who were familiar with formularies.

E. Comments from Survey Respondents

In this appendix, we provide selected comments that we received from survey respondents. The comments have been organized according to the topics discussed in Chapter 5 and are divided into three sections—general comments from direct-care system prescribers; comments from direct-care prescribers specifically in response to a question on changes they would make to the content, policies, and/or procedures of their MTF's formulary; and general comments from purchased-care system prescribers.

NOTE: Some of the comments listed in this appendix apply to more than one topic category, and therefore they appear more than once.

General Comments from Direct-Care System Prescribers

Pharmacy Staff

- [My MTF's] pharmacy is exemplary. They are attentive to the patient's time, restrictions, and physician prescribing habits, and go the extra mile to provide comprehensive reviews of efficacy and cost analysis prior to addition or deletion of any pharmacy item. Working with the constraints of funding and ability to provide, they graciously exhaust all their manpower. And may I say, they do it so gracefully. Never a complaint. Never a quiver.

- Our pharmacy staff is very approachable, friendly, and responds to all requests. We have our own pediatric pharmacy for non-controlled substances 8 to 4 Monday through Friday. The CHCS ORE system is wonderful. There is little or no difficulty in dealing with our pharmacy staff—they are very helpful. The only problem yet to be solved is the VERY long wait to have a prescription filled (up to three hours) at the main pharmacy. Automation improved this to 30 minutes, then it relapsed right back to horrible. We lose patients because of this and [because of limited] parking.

- I think our P&T committee does an excellent job with cost control but needs to communicate better with physicians so they are more a part of the process and not made to feel like their hands are being tied.

- Our pharmacy is top notch!

- Quicker pharmacy lines.

- The pharmacy is one of the *best* departments at my MTF.

- The formulary is NOT a problem. What is a problem is the chronic under-manning of our pharmacies. Those who are in our pharmacies are often poorly trained. If you want to do something useful for us providers, look at the manning of our pharmacies. I think you'd be shocked at the dangerous undermanning, which results in poor patient and provider satisfaction, increased errors, and patient harm.

- The main difficulty I have is in communications with the pharmacy—getting in touch with someone in the know about the formulary. Military pharmacists are quite busy, I know, but generally I can call a civilian pharmacy and, within a reasonable period of time, talk with the pharmacist for advice, availability of medication, etc. It is not so with the military pharmacies.

- As a provider and a customer/user of the system, I think it is much better than the outside civilian pharmacies.

- In general, I have been pleased with military pharmacy services.

Formulary Content

- The pharmacy is so slow to put LAWH on the formulary or drugs like Glitazone.

- Our pharmacy has been very receptive to the needs of the HIV-positive patients in keeping the latest antiretrovirals in stock.

- Make cold packs available to active duty [personnel] and dependents.

- I work at two area MTFs, geographically separated by approximately 30 miles. The formularies differ dramatically, and the rules regulating NMOP/local civilian pharmacy use and amounts of "chronic use" medicines given vary so dramatically that both doctors and patients find it confusing. Local P&T committees differ, and personal experience will often influence committee decisions. I feel policies and formularies should be standardized to the maximum extent, and the NMOP should provide variability and flexibility.

- On several occasions, medicines that are on our MTF formulary are not actually in the hospital. One of these medications was needed on an urgent basis. I have had to refer [patients] to a pharmacy outside the MTF because the medications were not available for over two weeks.

- Some formulary decisions are mandated by changes in the Triservice formulary. This can lead to changes that affect thousands, such as at our MTF.

- Suggest eliminating all OTCs [over-the counter medications] to decrease overall workload for providers and pharmacy.

- (1) One of the greatest problems is the frequent formulary changes. In my six-year cycle here, I have experienced [many] changes: These changes do not occur at the same time and require patient contact [simply] to change medications. Also, I get very offended as a board-certified internist when I am restricted from prescribing medications outside of my subspecialty. (2) Stop switching formulary drugs so often. (3) Don't switch brand names on patients' prescriptions (i.e., substituting one brand name or generic drug with another one when patients refill prescriptions).

Cost

- Reasonable cost containment has been abandoned at the provider level. Rather than a proper history and physical exam, unnecessary expensive testing is performed and unnecessary expensive drugs are prescribed (e.g., the emergency room will prescribe Ofloxacin at $0.97 per tab when Septra at $0.12 per tab will suffice. I find this offensive and the result of physician laziness.

- I have heard that the pharmacy budget drains our resources in the MTF due to the large number of prescriptions [that are] filled. Perhaps charging a co-pay on some or all medications would ease the financial burden. The co-pay could be minimal, e.g., $1.00.

- I attended P&T committee meetings when I first arrived here and became completely frustrated by the process, the lack of insight, the lack of willingness to listen to reason, the attitude that the job of the P&T committee and the formulary was to save the hospital's budget and discourage outside providers [from] writing the medications they desired for their patients. I have had my prescriptions changed by the pharmacy without my being informed—at the expense of the patient's health (this is practicing medicine without a license, as far as I'm concerned). Waiting time at any MTF for outpatient prescriptions, especially because of restrictions on the duration of prescriptions [is long], even for [medications for] chronic conditions that need to be refilled monthly; will not be dispensed [if the patient] shows up [two or three days early]—must be after 30 days.

154

Quality of Life

- Bigger hindrance is promotion. I will get out as soon as my 20 years are in. No problems in my files, just haven't done CGSC, which didn't use to be a requirement. Changing the rules in midstream is inappropriate. More and more administrative [hurdles].

- I am currently risking burnout with increased administrative demand and the increased number of patients I see. I am not sure how long this increased operational tempo can continue.

- We are doing more traveling to see patients at local clinics. Each local MTF formulary is different. We need to have a Triservice formulary that is the same for all local MTFs. MEDCEN formularies are more comprehensive and should also be equal at [all MTFs]. Many times, the electronic screens are not current. A drug will be listed as non-formulary, but when I call the pharmacy, the drug is on the shelf. Pharmacy courier services are provided from [my MTF] to [most MTFs in this area but not all]. This is inconvenient to patients [in those MTFs] who have to drive to [my MTF] to pick up a drug [their MTF] does not carry. Short of a special drug request, this decreases available manpower time due to patient travel time to pick up medications. Also, the local MTF pharmacies often cannot make an automatic refill number the default for certain drugs without going through [my MTF]; this is inconvenient. We waste time doing it manually each time we prescribe—carpal tunnel syndrome occurs!! Thanks for doing this. Hope this is helpful.

Outside Prescription/Pharmacy

- [My MTF] has done a very good job of balancing the many competing factors of funds, accessibility, and formulary. However, the outside prescriptions are a tremendous drain on dollars and create a vast drain on personnel resources and on parking within the facility. Again, outside prescriptions should go to outside-TRICARE no-co-payment pharmacies for TRICARE Prime patients and to co-pay [pharmacies] for non-Prime [patients].

- The MTF providers often have our prescriptions scrutinized more closely to [generate] cost savings to compensate for off-base Rxs that are cost inappropriate.

- Outside prescribers should have the same restrictions as military providers.

- Civilian providers seeing MTF beneficiaries outside the MTF tend to prescribe more expensive agents as first line [medications].

Quality of Care

- Overall, I think our pharmacy does an incredibly good job in meeting the medication needs of the patients. I think that patient satisfaction, and more than just monies, should impact the formulary. Also, patient compliance with daily medication is more apt to occur than with a cheaper QID [four times a day] medication, for example. Also, community standards need to be addressed, especially in oncology. If we can't prescribe Rituxan, even though it is FDA approved, we need to be able to refer patients to places where they can get life-saving treatments.

- Some formulary decisions are mandated by changes in the Triservice formulary. This can lead to changes that affect thousands, such as at our MTF.

- I attended P&T committee meetings when I first arrived here and became completely frustrated by the process, the lack of insight, the lack of willingness to listen to reason, the attitude that the job of the P&T committee and the formulary was to save the hospital's budget and discourage outside providers [from] writing the medications they desired for their patients. I have had my prescriptions changed by the pharmacy without my being informed—at the expense of the patient's health (this is practicing medicine without a license, as far as I'm concerned). Waiting time at any MTF for outpatient prescriptions, especially because of restrictions on the duration of prescriptions [is long], even for [medications for] chronic conditions that need to be refilled monthly; will not be dispensed [if the patient] shows up [two or three days early]—must be after 30 days.

- I think my patients have excellent pharmacy benefits, even though they may not appreciate it.

- Half of my time is spent with a fleet (ships assigned active duty). This population often has difficulty (still) obtaining their medications for six-month deployments—especially expensive prescriptions (regardless if it is a formulary or basic core formulary drug). This is an obstacle to care that must be eliminated. Our active duty fleet patients are why we exist. I have found that this large MTF is much more difficult to prescribe from than the medium-size MTF and branch medical clinic MTF that I have been assigned to, which I find interesting since they [the latter two] have more pharmacy budgetary constraints. I do not prescribe an outside provider's Rx and will not do so if I am not following the patient [over the course of] this diagnosis. I feel it is bad medical/prescriptive practice.

- The formulary is NOT a problem. What is a problem is the chronic under-manning of our pharmacies. Those who are in our pharmacies are often poorly trained. If you want to do something useful for us providers, look at the manning of our pharmacies. I think you'd be shocked at the dangerous undermanning, which results in poor patient and provider satisfaction, increased errors, and patient harm.

- We are doing more traveling to see patients at local clinics. Each local MTF formulary is different. We need to have a Triservice formulary that is the same for all local MTFs. MEDCEN formularies are more comprehensive and should also be equal at [all MTFs]. Many times, the electronic screens are not current. A drug will be listed as non-formulary, but when I call the pharmacy, the drug is on the shelf. Pharmacy courier services are provided from [my MTF] to [most MTFs in this area but not all]. This is inconvenient to patients [in those MTFs] who have to drive to [my MTF] to pick up a drug [their MTF] does not carry. Short of a special drug request, this decreases available manpower time due to patient travel time to pick up medications. Also, the local MTF pharmacies often cannot make an automatic refill number the default for certain drugs without going through [my MTF]; this is inconvenient. We waste time doing it manually each time we prescribe— carpal tunnel syndrome occurs!! Thanks for doing this. Hope this is helpful.

- Part of my time is spent with a small population of chronically ill pediatric young adult adolescent patients who are much healthier with the new medications that are available. These medications are very expensive but markedly improve quality and quantity of life. Our MTF has supported our availability of these medications after appropriate provision of the information on research showing the effectiveness [of these medications]. I am grateful on behalf of these patients.

Non-Formulary Approval Process

- There needs to be an expedited approval for "minor meds" that cost less than $20 to $30 per average prescription. This would allow more flexibility in adding/changing medications with little impact on overall cost.

- CHCS is an incredible help in prescribing for my patients. Overall, I am very pleased with the formulary and process to get non-formulary meds.

- The MTF pharmacy is generally accessible and willing to prescribe appropriate non-formulary medications.

- In my specialty practice, I am never denied medications that I have determined are most appropriate for my patients.

- I [utilize] mail order when drugs are expensive or not carried on our formulary.

Other/Miscellaneous

- [Respondent named two health plans] are the worst TRICARE contractors in terms of pharmacy benefits that I've experienced. Their first and only priority is to pinch the patients access to top-quality pharmaceuticals and frustrate providers trying to help the patient.

- I would love to have the PDR [Physician's Desk Reference] incorporated into CHCS so that it could be easily accessed without going out of the program.

- (1) The electronic prescribing on CHCS *can* be very helpful, especially in regard to allergies and interactions. *This* is a good feature. (2) Time is a big problem—15-minute appointments for geriatric patients on multiple medications means squeezed assessment time for medication review. (3) Formulary is a good idea and contains cost, but not enough physicians are consulted [on it].

- I think our pharmacy/formulary is a very reasonable one, and non-formulary requests, when reasonable, are handled positively and expeditiously. The single most frustrating aspect of my work is spending time on tasks which could/should be done by others—such as faxing, photocopying, and helping people get appointments—because the "system" is obstructive.

- While CHCS has been helpful, it has never been easy to determine which [drug] choices in a particular class were available.

- CHCS is getting more burdensome. More and more typing and sitting at the computer by physicians hurts patient care.

- As a specialist, I prescribe only the drugs that are my specialty and refer all other issues back to the primary care manager—hence, my knowledge of the "formulary" is really limited to the drugs I use for my scope of practice. Likewise, I request that those drugs that I feel necessary for my practice be added to the formulary. Therefore, all the questions you ask regarding my satisfaction or familiarity really reflect my or my colleague's endeavors to place whatever we need on the formulary.

Comments from Direct-Care System Prescribers in Response to Question on Recommended Changes to MTF Formulary

Question 18. If you had the opportunity, what changes would you make to the content, policies, and/or procedures of your MTF's formulary?

No Problems

- None. I think our system works quite well.

- Formulary is reasonable for my needs.

- None at this time. We have a pretty good system at present.

- I am basically satisfied with the contents of our formulary.

- No significant changes [to recommend].

- Our prescribing is all computer-based. All medications are labeled as formulary or non-formulary. Special drug requests are honored with reasonable speed and accuracy. The occasional glitch is [usually something like] a misplaced piece of paper when special requests are submitted.

- I have not encountered any roadblocks to prescribing medications at [my MTF]; however, my subspecialty has a narrow range of medications [that are] used.

- None. They have been very responsive.

- I have found that I can get almost any non-formulary drug my patients need by submitting a request and justifying the need of the medication.

- None.

- None presently.

- [My MTF] pharmacy is doing a good job of supplying medications requested. Non-stocked items are available to the patient in 24 to 48 hours. For the types of medications that I prescribe that are non-formulary, this has not created any detriment to the patients' health. A system is in place to automatically evaluate the addition of frequently requested non-formulary items to determine the advisability of adding them to the formulary. A non-formulary prescription requires a handwritten prescription that is signed by staff (trainees cannot sign). [Supervisory body] evaluates and educates providers on appropriate drug usage. This is the best system for meeting the needs of the patient and the provider that I have seen in 16 years of active duty.

- Have more personnel to run the pharmacy as they are overworked. Yet, despite all this, they've done an outstanding job!! It will also help the facility have a person working in the after-hours clinic.

- MTF is doing a fine job. When medical necessity dictates them, drugs have been obtained.

- I feel that our pharmacist and P&T committee do an excellent job of supporting provider ordering. Have no complaints with present system.

- I am satisfied as they are now.

- No change. Pharmacy is doing an excellent job.

- None—works well as is with minimal problems.

Cost

- Drop expensive drugs that have no therapeutic advantage, e.g. (1) Ortho 777 is more than $15 per pack versus Trileven at $1.25 per pack; (2) Preman is $0.22 per tab versus Estrace at $0.02 per tab. Stop pharmacy rep visits to physicians.

- For higher-priced medications, I have a comment about possible cheaper alternatives. [Respondent listed several alternative medications in the write-in section of the survey.]

- Have an automatic annual review by pharmacy and medical department of medications for addition or deletion from the pharmacy. Currently, it occurs every few years. To protect the MTF budget and expand the formulary, I would like to see all outside prescriptions filled by TRICARE (private) pharmacies or by the mail order national pharmacy—with no co-pay for TRICARE prime but co-pay for non-prime.

- Have retail cost of drug printed out at the time the medication is dispensed. This may educate patients about actual costs, may cut down on waste, and may inspire patients to appreciate their pharmacy benefits.

- Requests for non-formulary items are taking up to a month at present to be processed! This is a change from the previous four to five days. This is burdensome for the patient and doctor. This process needs to be facilitated! Increase education on pharmaceutical costs and pricing.

- Prefer that when formulary changes are made, everyone is not forced to use a new drug if the old drug is working. It seems penny wise and pound foolish to subject thousands of patients to a different drug if their previous prescription worked well. It generates a lot of visits, phone calls, and confusion. [It also generates] repeated lab tests and [there could be] additional side effects (i.e., with Lipitor versus Baycol; Prevacid versus Protonix).

- Non-TRICARE beneficiaries pharmacy budget should not come out of MTF money. This places a burden on the MTF to not add new drugs to the formulary due to concerns of misuse by civilian providers locally. In the end, TRICARE Prime beneficiaries suffer due to restrictive formulary policies that cannot control civilian prescribing patterns!

- Develop a policy by which a patient pays the difference in the cost of a drug if a formulary alternative exists but the patient demands [the drug] anyway.

- Increase the pharmacy budget to allow physicians to prescribe more current, proven, state-of-the-art medications.

- Encourage drug companies to offer better discounts on drugs.

- I would be interested in knowing how much money is spent on OTC medications prescribed.

- More money!

- If the DoD mandates that the MTF must fill all prescriptions presented by outside providers, then the DoD should fund the MTF to cover the expense.

- Capitated costs to my MTF severely hamper my ability to practice medicine as compared with a large tertiary center.

- Cost is not the bottom line at all times.

- Pharmacists' role is only to give pharmacologic and cost information, not guidelines on use.

- Pharmacy funding DoD-wide needs to be worked out so that [the MTFs] are not always "going under" at the end of the fiscal year.

- Filling outside scripts has made the MTF formulary more "restrictive"— expensive drugs such as Cox 2's are "available" only through NDRs (new drug requests). To place [such a drug] "in formulary" opens it to all, and the outside providers may not be following our guidelines. Our MTF has at least "streamlined" the process and has made it relatively easy to submit NDRs. Patients in our system do not have any incentive to help contain cost—the providers are sandwiched in between the patients demanding the "new drug" and the pharmacy demanding cost be contained; a co-pay system would help this.

- No closed categories; better funding.

- Cost comparison analysis across a class of drugs such as AEM (including medication costs and lab tests needed, as well as [costs arising from] complications), as well as efficacy comparison [are recommended].

Non-Formulary Issues

- The oversight for special purchase/non-formulary items is too strict. Other than that, I think we have an outstanding formulary and pharmacy staff.

- A DoD formulary is a good goal, but the newer drugs should be obtained by the requesting provider until the type of drugs in a class has a track record.

- I usually don't get notified if a non-formulary drug is denied until the angry patient calls. Need more feedback from pharmacy.

- I understand the need for cost containment but feel that if there is a medicine that better suits a patient, it should be easily accessible. While the process has been improved, I feel it still has too much red tape binding the providers' hands.

- Less administrative [procedures] to get non-formulary drugs.

- Requests for non-formulary items are taking up to a month at present to be processed! This is a change from the previous four to five days. This is burdensome for the patient and doctor. This process needs to be facilitated! Increase education on pharmaceutical costs and pricing.

- A formulary in hard copy. Update to new medications on the market. Less hard copy paperwork for non-formulary drug.

- Simply, if a drug is truly required clinically and is not formulary, the approval process should be simpler and more streamlined.

- Publish an updated formulary on the Web every month that is easy to look up, especially by drug classes and therapeutic categories. Allow "key access" to "restrictive drugs" universally to the most senior staff.

- I would distribute the minutes of meetings to providers along with regularly scheduled updates of formulary change. Would review policies regarding the process for requests from specialty clinics for non-formulary prescribing. At our facility, the number of subspecialty clinics with the ability to prescribe Vioxx is so large that they can't fit the list [of subspecialty clinics] on a single line. Patients are inappropriately placed on [Vioxx] and then expect us to continue prescribing it.

- [The pharmacy should] have cardiac medications that are supported by evidence-based medical efficiencies, regardless of cost.

- Make changes to non-formulary MTF drugs available electronically, as long as they are electronically signed by a staff physician (not resident/intern/trainee). Why? Because most non-formulary drug requests are not denied, you might as well do them electronically and allow any denials to occur electronically to provide feedback to the provider.

- Some drugs are placed on special order status only to restrict their use, even though the P&T committee knows their use is justified in some cases. Doing a special drug request for these [special orders] is annoying.

- Decrease the amount of time taken to process a new drug request. Some medications I requested be added to formulary, which I routinely use (e.g., DDAVP nasal spray/tablets for bed-wetting), were denied for cost issues or alternative forms (e.g., Claritin tablets were denied even though we have Claritin liquid on formulary), so I have to write civilian prescriptions for [Claratin tablets], which I assume cost more. But overall I am a member of our P&T committee and very pleased with the overall responsiveness to cover newer, more-effective medications even though it may be more costly.

- The problem is NOT the formulary. We have a retrospective review process for non-formulary requests. Thus, the patient is never kept waiting while approval is obtained. The prescribing physician is the approval authority. The P&T committee reviews non-formulary requests after the fact to identify [questionable] provider patterns. This process has not been abused by our providers. Also, if a non-formulary drug is being ordered by multiple providers on a routine basis, this medication is automatically discussed at P&T [committee meetings] for possible addition to the formulary. Prospective review of non-formulary requests is irritating to providers and has the potential to harm patients. It should be eliminated throughout the Navy.

- The ordering of non-formulary items at [my MTF] is very easy, but there is still a three- to five-day delay in starting [these prescriptions]. So, I just send [the orders] downtown. I wish we could shorten the time to med to one day.

- Not having to resubmit special requests for "off-formulary" drugs that are refills.

- Most frustrating are the irrational restrictions on my prescribing practice. Fully certified M.D.'s should not be held to same restrictions as physician's assistant's, nurse practitioners, and other non-M.D. providers!! I am a board-certified pediatrician and am fully trained to prescribe medications for reflux, asthma, allergies, antibiotics, etc. At [my MTF], I am unable to prescribe many of these drugs without specialty approval. Also, Zyrtec standard dosing is one-half tab per day, which is ineffective for many and not what is recommended by the manufacturer. The acne medications and eczema topicals that are available are inadequate at best, and many of the useful products that I use in my private practice I have to refer my military patients to dermatology or allergy [specialists] or send [them] to an outside pharmacy.

- I am a primary care provider. I am restricted from prescribing medications for common medical problems because they can only be prescribed by specialists (e.g., Vioxx, risedronate, Celexa, Lamictal). Therefore, in order to refill or prescribe these medications, I am forced to send [patients]to a specialist or write a non-formulary drug request. This is frustrating to me because my prescribing patterns are actually more cost conscious than those of most specialists and [this process] requires more visits and more time spent per patient.

- I believe physicians should be able to prescribe what they deem best suits their patients. I try to use cheaper agents first, but I should be given more freedom to switch [based] on my clinical judgment.

- Decrease the time and paperwork associated with prescribing non-formulary drugs.

Formulary Content

- Maybe consider adding some pediatric preparations.

- Add Lipitor. Certainly a pharmacy committee that does not have physician/nurse practitioner representation for an MTF should not be allowed to make changes to the formulary. And at least, any proposed changes should be distributed to ALL providers in that MTF PRIOR to the changes being made.

- Add glucosmine and chondroifin sulfate.

- We need to re-examine the choice of antibiotics we are carrying; update them with much better pediatric choices. Need to be able to make changes in a more time-efficient manner.

- My biggest complaint is how difficult it is to add or change a formulary item. It takes several hours of my time to write up/type the request (I have no secretary who can do it). I have to cancel clinic time to attend the P&T committee meeting. Most times, the request is denied the first time around. I have to get more supporting data and return to the P&T committee. This is a time-consuming process that takes a concerted effort over several months to add or change one medication. Often that [process] provides only a "trial period," and I have to return with more data to justify final approval. This is true for all medications—there is no easy way for me to get experience with a new therapy. NDRs require me to fill out the form, submit it, wait to hear if it is approved, and wait to get a message that the medication is available, and then I have to enter the prescription and personally call the patients so they can pick up the Rx. This process is so burdensome that I almost never try new acne creams or other advances, and as a result my patients "get by" with older therapies. No doubt the hospital saves money by keeping the system burdensome for the providers. I wish I could give out samples, like all other dermatologists.

- Stop the frequent changes to formulary. I often have to change a patient's Rx about once a year to adjust for formulary shifts and not for medical reasons.

- Add Lipitor back to the formulary; the automatic switch caused loss of control of lipids (in previously controlled population), more monitoring costs, and a lot more provider time to check LTTs and monitor previously stable lipids. (Baycol is not as effective.)

- More choices for hormone replacement therapy.

- Add Cox-2 NSAIDS.

- Don't know. I am satisfied with what we have, although the formulary could be more complete and current.

- As a dermatologist: (1) I would add Differin Gel (Adapolene); (2) I would add a quality sun block to use in high risk patients; (3)I would add Valtrex to treatment for Herpes Zoster and herpes simplex virus [HSV].

- I would distribute the minutes of meetings to providers along with regularly scheduled updates of formulary change. Would review policies regarding the process for requests from specialty clinics for non-formulary prescribing. At our facility, the number of subspecialty clinics with the ability to prescribe Vioxx is so large that they can't fit the list [of subspecialty clinics] on a single line. Patients are inappropriately placed on [Vioxx] and then expect us to continue prescribing it.

- Add Suprax liquid; add Vasotec.

- Easier availability of Viagra, when clinically indicated.

- I have not encountered any roadblocks to prescribing medications at [my MTF]; however, my subspecialty has a narrow range of medications [that are] used.

- I think our system works well and is responsive to the requests of physicians and the needs of patients. In a perfect world, there would be no budgeting limitations, and I could prescribe any brand of medication I wanted (any type of growth hormone, for instance). Also, it would be nice to hand out some OTC items (e.g., alcohol swabs, etc.). What is challenging here is that there are four to six different facilities on the same computer system, but their formulary contents are all different!

- [The pharmacy should] have cardiac medications that are supported by evidence-based medical efficiencies, regardless of cost.

- Quicker addition to the formulary of medication on the market that civilian providers use to practice [their] standard of care.

- I would revamp the entire formulary to begin with, acquiring a list from providers of the medications they WANT to prescribe, with justifications. Emphasize the cost-savings to the U.S. Army that would be realized by purchasing and prescribing through the MTF, rather than through NMOP or outside pharmacies. Make those cost savings available as increased pharmacy budget monies to the MTFs.

- Take ALL over-the-counter medications off the formulary! Placing orders for these is a big waste of provider time!

- Discontinue all OTC products and unproven remedies.

- Addition of a Cox-2 Inhibitor and Viagra.

- If you can justify stocking the pill form, it seems a bit schizophrenic not to stock the liquid form for patients (i.e., children) who can't swallow pills (for example, biasin).

- Larger selection of clinically effective meds with different dosing options, such as once a day instead of four times a day, rather than basing selections of drugs solely on costs.

- Increase variety and patient options.

- No closed categories; better funding.

- None. Possibly quit supplying OTC meds to save money.

- Make formularies within different military MTFs consistent. [My MTF] pharmacy carries different ACE [angiotensin converting enzyme] than [other MTFs within the same system]. This makes it difficult to prescribe medications for patients to pick up at other sites.

Patient Issues

- Make prescribing policies clear to patients.

- While avoiding "fads," it is important to update available treatments for chronic illness (i.e., diabetes or HIV).

- Once a patient is on a certain medication and it's working, and both the patient and physician are satisfied, then the patient's medication should not be changed to another drug in the formulary, even if the new drug is equally effective.

166

Process

- I usually don't get notified if a non-formulary drug is denied until the angry patient calls. Need more feedback from pharmacy.

- Reduce redundant paperwork!

- Currently, we use electronic prescribing via CHCS. This works adequately and is fairly easy for me to tell what is on formulary and what isn't while prescribing. The one thing that could improve it would be a more friendly user interface! (This is a CHCS-wide problem, not one limited to formulary or prescribing concerns, however.)

- Not having to deal with DoD mail-order system—took two hours for them to fax me forms!!

- Allow optimization of CHCS so that I may be allowed to order a prescription for a beneficiary from another MTF within our region, allowing me to choose the MTF easily within CHCS. The pharmacies within our region and DoD have suboptimal reimbursement practices.

- Choose a single mechanism for prescribing all non-formulary drugs. [Now, the] procedures for approval change based upon which drug is involved. Procedures seem to vary even with the same drug from week to week. I end up completing all possible procedures/forms to ensure medication is approved. I am also provided with little feedback to know if medication is approved or not. I assume no news is good news!!

- Prefer that when formulary changes are made, everyone is not forced to use a new drug if the old drug is working. It seems penny wise and pound foolish to subject thousands of patients to a different drug if their previous prescription worked well. It generates a lot of visits, phone calls, and confusion. [It also generates] repeated lab tests and [there could be] additional side affects (i.e., with Lipitor versus Baycol; Prevacid versus Protonix).

- Renewal of current prescriptions works well. I wish renewal of expired or discontinued prescriptions could be retrieved and renewed as easily rather than having to generate a new Rx in CHCS.

- Not certain why the day's supply and quantity are not linked in an Rx. Many inpatients receive Rx on discharge with two-weeks' supply with refills, but are unable to get the refills because the phone-in refill [service person] thinks it's a 30-day supply and [the refills] are denied. This generates a lot of extra work and/or the patients stop using the medication because they had trouble refilling it.

- Our formulary should be listed by drug category with the preferred (low-cost) drug listed first over less-preferred (high-cost) drug. For example, I could type in "anti-depressant" and gets lists of SSRIs [selective serotonin reuptake inhibitors], tricyclics, MAO [inhibitors], and then click on SSRI and see a list with Paxil, Prozac, and Zoloft with their relative costs. It is difficult to find what drugs are on a formulary by classes. There are times when patients have requested medications, and I have had them filled outside the MTF even though they have recently been added on our formulary [because they were added] without my knowledge.

- When new drugs are established as the drug of choice for certain classes, policies for automatic substitution should be instituted for appropriate patient education. This responsibility should fall to the MTF and not the individual provider.

- The electronic (CHCS) formulary is not user friendly. We should be able to type a category and get options. If a drug is not on the formulary, we should be told the alternatives.

- Quicker addition to the formulary of medication on the market that civilian providers use to practice [their] standard of care.

- The only difficulty is when a given drug in a particular class is the "preferred" drug for a while (like Zyctec), only to be replaced by something else (like Allegra) as the preferred drug. I am not going to change all the medications for patients who are doing well on the original.

- Evaluate the necessity of having new medications [that are] more efficacious, on the formulary, especially if the patient has tried other medications and [they are] not helping.

- Pharmacy and Therapeutics [committee] should get input from the specialist for adding or deleting medicines.

- Eliminate unnecessary drugs (now being done here) and unavailable drugs.

- Easier access to new drugs and have them added to the formulary more quickly.

- Have more physician involvement in order to integrate clinical and patient care concerns. I find it offensive that pharmacists are controlling my prescribing activities and limiting my practice of medicine by instituting narrow-minded and dogmatic pharmacy protocols. "Value" in your questionnaire is assumed to denote dollars. There is more to medicine than money. I am able to stay within the confines of our formulary most of the time, but my choice to prescribe outside that formulary should not be

168

bureaucratically challenged, especially by pharmacists and non-clinical personnel.

- Combine the formularies in the National Capitol Area. Patients should be able to visit the closest MTF and get refills or new prescriptions.

- Cut back on non-Prime prescriptions from non-MTF (civilian) providers.

- Electronic requests for non-formulary drugs.

- Removal of OTCs or OTCs available to patients without a prescription.

- Allow SPP medication requests to be filled at satellite clinics for the patient's convenience.

- DoD should have one formulary—most conversions are started due to [transfers] from one MTF to another.

- Make it easier to add medication to the formulary.

- (1) Standardize the process. (2) Different medications [should not] require different forms. (3) Pharmacy never gives the patient the form, so I have to try to find one. Clinic does not always have one. (4) Sometimes I'm not sure what form is needed.

- Need more coordination of formularies in the National Capitol Area (Washington, D.C.) between the Air Force, Army, and Navy. Particularly for consultants, it can be difficult to care for people if they can't get a drug refilled at their local MTF and have to get it at consultant's MTF only or [through a] civilian source.

- (1) Get rid of OTCs—patients waste valuable appointment slots for "refills" of OTCs. (2) DoD should allow for samples—it's the only way we can gain experience with new drugs.

- [There should be] electronic processing of "special drug requests." These requests [now] require the physician to hand-carry the form through the approval process or [else] it gets left on someone's desk indefinitely.

- Better, searchable drug database with classes of drugs and costs available [in the database]. Needs to be quick and easy to use.

- (1) Updated formulary. (2) Updated computer program for prescribing.

- Computerized formulary with drug class groups.

Rules/Restrictions

- Lessen the number of restrictions.

- Remove specialty restrictions for some drugs and place such drugs under request for approval by specialist.

- Disallow Rx by civilian providers of patients who are *not* TRICARE Prime.

- Non-TRICARE beneficiaries' pharmacy budget should not come out of MTF money. This places a burden on the MTF to not add new drugs to the formulary due to concerns of misuse by civilian providers locally. In the end, TRICARE Prime beneficiaries suffer due to restrictive formulary policies that cannot control civilian prescribing patterns!

- Restrict less medications to specific services. Rather, educate providers in regard to cost, side effects, and appropriate use. Give feedback as needed to providers in regard to their use of expensive/third-line medications.

- Don't block any Rx from specialists, only family doctors.

- I would allow certain medications to be restricted by specialty. This would prevent overutilization of some expensive medications by providers who might not have the training to appropriately prescribe certain medications. [But it would still] allow the specialist the ease of routine prescription writing rather than going through the non-formulary approval process.

- Certain drugs are controlled by the pharmacy by permitting only certain subspecialists to use them. Examples include sumatriptan, mirtazapine, and celecoxib. I find this more exasperating than obtaining a new drug order request to circumvent restrictions on non-formulary drugs. If these drugs are to be tried on a trial basis, a consult [to a specialist] has to be generated.

- Less restriction of prescribing (i.e., specialists only prescribing for Vioxx or Metrogel is ridiculous).

- Restrict beneficiaries with non-MTF prescriptions from using MTF pharmacy. Require that they use the non-MTF options that are now widely available. That would allow the MTF formulary to expand without the concern that the budget would go out of control because of prescriptions by non-MTF providers.

- Do not restrict drugs to specific specialties.

- Restricting drugs to subspecialists results in consults to them that may be unnecessary (for asthma and allergy medications in particular).

- The formulary in "theory" is fine. A problem occurs if you need to step outside the formulary. Many times I have experienced the attitude from pharmacy staff and commanders that [they think] I don't know what I'm doing. As a result, many requests get denied. The main concern seems to be money, and only "lip service" is given to quality/standard of care. Pharmacy policies are only one of the many reasons I am leaving the DoD.

- Most frustrating are the irrational restrictions on my prescribing practice. Fully certified M.D.'s should not be held to same restrictions as physician's assistant's, nurse practitioners and other non-M.D. providers!! I am a board-certified pediatrician and am fully trained to prescribe meds for reflux, asthma, allergies, antibiotics, etc. At [my MTF], I am unable to prescribe many of these drugs without specialty approval. Also, Zyrtec standard dosing is one-half tab per day, which is ineffective for many and not what is recommended by the manufacturer. The acne medications and eczema topicals that are available are inadequate at best, and many of the useful products that I use in my private practice I have to refer my military patients to dermatology or allergy [specialists] or send [them] to an outside pharmacy.

- I am a primary care provider. I am restricted from prescribing medications for common medical problems because they can only be prescribed by specialists (e.g., Vioxx, risedronate, Celexa, Lamictal). Therefore, in order to refill or prescribe these medications, I am forced to send [patients]to a specialist or write a non-formulary drug request. This is frustrating to me because my prescribing patterns are actually more cost conscious than those of most specialists and [this process] requires more visits and more time spent per patient.

- Avoid prescriber limitations for refills—some drugs are limited-prescription medications, limited to specific subspecialists. When I try to help a patient with a refill, I am blocked [from doing so], and the patient must contact the sub-specialist.

Communication

- Make prescribing policies clear to patients.

- I usually don't get notified if a non-formulary drug is denied until the angry patient calls. Need more feedback from pharmacy.

- After each P&T committee meeting, e-mail to ORE a list reporting the summary actions taken/considered. Actually, it would be good for all committees to have a brief summary reported to the affected community after each meeting. Communication always enhances function.

- A formulary in hard copy. Update to new medications on the market. Less hard copy paperwork for non-formulary drugs.

- Our formulary should be listed by drug category with the preferred (low-cost) drug listed first over less-preferred (high-cost) drugs. For example, I could type in "anti-depressant" and gets lists of SSRIs [selective serotonin reuptake inhibitors], tricyclics, MAO [inhibitors], and then click on SSRI and see a list with Paxil, Prozac, and Zoloft with their relative costs. It is difficult to find what drugs are on a formulary by classes. There are times when patients have requested medications, and I have had them filled outside the MTF even though they have recently been added on our formulary [because they were added] without my knowledge.

- Publish an updated formulary on the Web every month that is easy to look up, especially by drug classes and therapeutic categories. Allow "key access" to "restrictive drugs" universally to the most senior staff.

- I would distribute the minutes of meetings to providers along with regularly scheduled updates of formulary change. Would review policies regarding the process for requests from specialty clinics for non-formulary prescribing. At our facility, the number of subspecialty clinics with the ability to prescribe Vioxx is so large that they can't fit the list [of subspecialty clinics] on a single line. Patients are inappropriately placed on [Vioxx] and then expect us to continue prescribing it.

- The electronic (CHCS) formulary is not user friendly. We should be able to type a category and get options. If a drug is not on the formulary, we should be told the alternatives.

- Currently at my facility, there is no list. The only way to see if a drug is on formulary is to try to order it and see if it is there. An actual listing would be helpful.

- Make changes to non-formulary MTF drugs available electronically, as long as they are electronically signed by a staff physician (not resident/intern/trainee). Why? Because most non-formulary drug requests are not denied, you might as well do them electronically and allow any denials to occur electronically to provide feedback to the provider.

- More information on the cost of drugs versus alternative drugs within the same class.

- Updating *printed* formulary would be helpful—can better see the big picture. Online CHCS drug data are fine. Sometimes I'm unaware of treatment options and relative costs within a drug category. This needs to be in print form.

- It would be beneficial to have a hard copy of the most current formulary and key policies for prescribing medications at the MTF. These vary from place to

172

place, and now in large MTFs many things are left to the provider to figure out as they go along. Not everyone in the facility has easy access to the pharmacy Web page. In addition, things out of stock or changes are not sent to the provider via CHCS e-mail. Again, one finds out through department meetings or [when] trying to order things.

- Make the formulary readily available, either printed or electronic, with updates of drug preparations and dosage strengths available.

- Notification of medical house staff prior to removal of drugs from the formulary to generate feedback and practical discussion of implications and alternative agents (with the overall goal of maintaining optimal patient care).

- (1) Publish regularly in electronic/Web and printed formats. (2) Allow visualization of all drugs in one class in CHCS. (3) Notification to physician that special medication is not only approved (we receive this [in a timely fashion now] through CHCS SPP requests), but that the medication has been obtained and "delivered" to patient.

- (1) Open format for all physicians to have input (*not* just the director). (2) Regular meetings with pharmacist. (3) Dissemination of information to patients on why certain drugs are included or excluded. (4) Better feedback when requesting non-formulary drugs. (5) Provide prescribing patterns through quarterly reports.

- Give feedback on commonly prescribed non-formulary medicines. Trends may indicate a need to amend the formulary.

- Better, searchable drug database with classes of drugs and costs available [in the database]. Needs to be quick and easy to use.

- Just send out updated formulary drug lists. Also, directions on the correct procedure to acquire non-formulary medications if needed.

- Please provide current hard copy formulary book on all drugs in our formulary plus a field-specific one as well. Local MTFs in our area all have different formularies, making it hard [for doctors] to know what's available when they travel to local MTFs or staff clinics. We need to be on the same formulary. Too much time is wasted in seeing what is available at a given MTF.

- Remind providers about the non-formulary process; update [the physician/prescriber] on additions via CHCS.

Miscellaneous

- Better responsiveness and pro-activeness regarding the Advance Practice Nurse's formulary.

- Weighted criteria list.

- Hiring more pharmacy personnel to cover the after-hours clinic will help the providers to better concentrate on the patient care instead of dispensing actual (limited) medications, thereby reducing errors, which are increasing because of the pressure!!

- I do not agree with the policies on the HMG-CoA reductace inhibitors statins.

General Comments from Purchased-Care System Prescribers

Pharmacy Issues

- It would be nice for the patients if I could call or fax in prescriptions. The local MTFs accept only written prescriptions. I don't think it could be too hard to change this policy, and it would make it more convenient for the patient.

- I am very unhappy with the fact that the military base does not provide a copy of a formulary. I cannot prescribe medications on the formulary if I do not have knowledge of what is on the formulary! Furthermore, it is almost impossible to get any help by phoning them. They will not allow refills by phone or fax like real pharmacies. My patients are very upset when they drive 30-plus miles to the base to fill a prescription and are told that the prescription is not on their formulary. In my opinion, it is a poor excuse for a pharmacy, but I guess that the price is right!

- Frustration is sometimes expressed [by patients] that [their] prescriptions cannot be filled 100 percent on base.

- Having an in-house pharmacy that accepts TRICARE is very helpful. The formulary from the local MTF is readily available and helps with prescribing.

Insurance Burden (Formulary Burden)

- We participate in 30 different insurance plans. It is impossible or at least very impractical to keep track of the insurance plans' formularies because of the extra time involved. We already spend as much time with insurance paperwork as we do providing medical care and would actively resist any additional regulatory burden.

- I find it impossible to keep up with formularies, as we see patients from so many plans and have little time to track down formularies, look up drugs, and such. I write prescriptions with no regard to what may or may not be on a formulary, and let the pharmacist call me if there is a problem.

- Medicine, in general, is becoming less and less attractive due to insurance and medication dictates, hassles, and constraints. I think many physicians would retire ASAP if they had the means. I still enjoy my work, but probably less so than five years ago. I was planning on working into my 70s, but I am now reconsidering. I feel our medical system is really broken, and the [broken] pieces multiply each year.

- Formularies are basically a good idea; however, with the large number of insurers each having a formulary, to look up the prescriptions on every patient is time consuming and therefore not done. Additionally, when considering medications on formularies, frequently medications available for one-to-two times a day dosing are left off in favor of four-times-a-day cheaper medications. Few people take [medications] four times a day, [which] minimizes the therapeutic effect. Dosing frequency or ease of administration must be considered an important factor when generating formularies.

- It is difficult to keep up with all the insurance companies' formularies. I always ask my patients if they know if a certain medication is available at [the MTF]. I do sign all of my prescriptions on the "product selection permitted" side [of the prescription form]; however, this seems unacceptable at the [MTF]. By signing this, it should allow the pharmacist to make the substitution. I don't have this problem with commercial pharmacies.

- Patients are on health insurance plans that keep changing periodically, and formulary lists also keep changing very frequently. Given the immense number of plans that our staff has to deal with, it is very difficult to check on formulary plans every time one writes a prescription. Besides, patients who have used a certain medication for many months (in some cases for years) should not be changing their medications.

- I suppose formularies are a necessary evil to contain costs. I find them, however, to be extremely burdensome. Most of my TRICARE patients have the mindset, "If I can't get it for free (or very cheap), I don't want it." I try to prescribe the best and safest medicine, which at times means it is more expensive. I would like to see doing away with blanket rejections and onerous obstacles. Instead, [I would like to see] a tiered system where the patients can still get what is best and safest for them just by paying a bit higher co-pay. Then, I would have to do fewer unnecessary lab tests and additional office visits, [and I would have] fewer hoops to jump through. Bureaucrats don't know why a certain medication is best for a certain patient. They don't know the long history of what has been tried and failed or associated with side effects already. I do.

- I usually don't have time to consider a patient's insurance during our encounters. I will often ask the drug reps if their products are on all the formularies or not. If one formulary doesn't cover [a drug], I tend not to use it because I can't keep track of all the different lists. Also, because I practice in a group, I may not be the one who has to change a medication because it isn't on the formulary. The pharmacist may speak to a nurse who "runs it by" another doctor. Even if a drug is the most cost effective in its class, it may not work well for an individual. There needs to be more leeway [in what we can prescribe].

- Formulary/preferred drug programs are a pain!! Busy practices with contracts with multiple insurance programs/health care systems are overwhelmed with drug formulary/preferred lists (our practice [has] over 30 [contracts]); it is impossible to keep up. Additionally, most [plans] routinely deny appropriate drug coverage.

- Formularies and tiered systems are *very* cumbersome for the practitioner. We see many insurance company patients and many formularies, which seem to change all the time.

- A burden is placed on physicians by faxed letters of rejection to switch brands of medication to "formulary"[medications]. However, a better idea is to have patients know about alternative brands and let them decide on trying a new agent (often when the incentive is the money that could be saved). Being a middle person between insurance [companies] and patients is difficult. If the insurance plan wants to save money with the patient's OK, then approval by the physician would be appropriate and time saving.

- Generally, I feel that formularies are useful for insurance companies. However, in a busy practice, it is very time consuming to check formularies for each prescription. We care for patients [covered by] most insurance companies. Plus, every patient has his or her own preferences, effectiveness profiles, etc.

Quality of Life

- Medicine, in general, is becoming less and less attractive due to insurance and medication dictates, hassles, and constraints. I think many physicians would retire ASAP if they had the means. I still enjoy my work, but probably less so than five years ago. I was planning on working into my 70s, but I am now reconsidering. I feel our medical system is really broken, and the [broken] pieces multiply each year.

- I am made bitter by the over-regulation; it is an abuse of our profession! When I go through a medical process, I want my decision to be respected as it is!

- Since EMTALA [Emergency Medical Treatment and Active Labor Act] has made emergency physicians the only legally mandated slave labor in the United States, there are far too many rules, regulations, formularies, and contracts we are supposed to be familiar with, and not enough hours in the day.

Cost

- We are frustrated by TRICARE's abysmal reimbursement. Most doctors in this geographic area are not [TRICARE] providers because of this. We fought with TRICARE over depoprovera coverage. I have to buy 96 units of depo to get the lowest price of $41.20 each. TRICARE pays $45 plus $12 copay. What business can survive with such a narrow profit margin? TRICARE is the worst payer for depoprovera. [TRICARE] used to pay $31 [each], and I almost dropped my provider status over this. I feel military personnel should get the drugs prescribed at no cost to them. When I was in active duty, I served in the P&T committee and we were responsive to patient needs and costs; it worked well. But managed care P&T committees are dishonest, and I cannot deal with the myriad formularies shoved my way. I have never seen a TRICARE formulary.

- Drug costs are very, very important and need to be contained because they are driving the increasing cost of medical care. On the other hand, drug companies would not increasingly be coming out with truly miraculous, new, and safer medications if they didn't think they could make large profits [after] the tremendous costs of R&D and going through the FDA approval process. I don't know the correct balance of these two important aspects of the problem.

- To get quality physicians to this area, where the population is significantly military related, the emphasis has to shift from discounted fee for service to quality physicians (specialty based, board certified). With the emphasis on discounted fee for service, it is difficult to recruit quality physicians. This is a disservice to not only the CHAMPUS beneficiaries but also the community at large. Quality physicians cost less [in the long run] by providing better care. Especially now that TRICARE payments [are more] in line with Medicare rates, the system should move away from who-gives-more-of-a-discount to who-are-the-better-physicians.

- TRICARE patients are a welcome addition to our practice! Due to exceptionally low reimbursements in the other plans, we can only accept TRICARE Standard. To expand patients' opportunity for quality care and resources, [TRICARE should] consider raising reimbursements in a competitive marketplace.

- I don't have a problem with a tiered co-pay for medications, but I have a real problem with a formulary that won't pay any of the cost of a medication when other less-expensive medications have been tried and failed. The main examples are Concerta or Metadate, Adderall, Diflucan, Xapenex, and Pulmicort (not just with TRICARE, but in general), and some formularies won't pay for any antidepressants that I prescribe for my adolescent patients; [then] the patient has to see a psychiatrist.

- Patients need to be *educated* as to (a) why they have a formulary and (b) what the cost of their *medications* is. They are currently too removed from the true cost of their health care, including drug costs.

- Most patients confuse *price* (cost) with *value.*

Formulary Content

- We are frustrated by TRICARE's abysmal reimbursement. Most doctors in this geographic area are not [TRICARE] providers because of this. We fought with TRICARE over depoprovera coverage. I have to buy 96 units of depo to get the lowest price of $41.20 each. TRICARE pays $45 plus $12 copay. What business can survive with such a narrow profit margin? TRICARE is the worst payer for depoprovera. [TRICARE] used to pay $31 [each], and I almost dropped my provider status over this. I feel military personnel should get the drugs prescribed at no cost to them. When I was in active duty, I served in the P&T committee and we were responsive to patient needs and costs; it worked well. But managed care P&T committees are dishonest, and I cannot deal with the myriad formularies shoved my way. I have never seen a TRICARE formulary.

- As a fertility specialist, it does not make sense to me that TRICARE patients can have certain fertility drugs or treatment only if they are seen at a base facility. The drugs should be covered wherever the patient is seen if they need it.

- I don't have a problem with a tiered co-pay for medications, but I have a real problem with a formulary that won't pay any of the cost of a medication when other less-expensive medications have been tried and failed. The main examples are Concerta or Metadate, Adderall, Diflucan, Xapenex, and Pulmicort (not just with TRICARE, but in general), and some formularies won't pay for any antidepressants that I prescribe for my adolescent patients; [then] the patient has to see a psychiatrist.

- I usually don't have time to consider a patient's insurance during our encounters. I will often ask the drug reps if their products are on all the formularies or not. If one formulary doesn't cover [a drug], I tend not to use it because I can't keep track of all the different lists. Also, because I practice in a group, I may not be the one who has to change a medication because it isn't on the formulary. The pharmacist may speak to a nurse who "runs it by" another doctor. Even if a drug is the most cost effective in its class, it may not work well for an individual. There needs to be more leeway [in what we can prescribe].

Quality of Care

- To get quality physicians to this area, where the population is significantly military related, the emphasis has to shift from discounted fee for service to quality physicians (specialty based, board certified). With the emphasis on discounted fee for service, it is difficult to recruit quality physicians. This is a disservice to not only the CHAMPUS beneficiaries but also the community at large. Quality physicians cost less [in the long run] by providing better care. Especially now that TRICARE payments [are more] in line with Medicare rates, the system should move away from who-gives-more-of-a-discount to who-are-the-better-physicians.

- Patients are on health insurance plans that keep changing periodically, and formulary lists also keep changing very frequently. Given the immense number of plans that our staff has to deal with, it is very difficult to check on formulary plans every time one writes a prescription. Besides, patients who have used a certain medication for many months (in some cases for years) should not be changing their medications.

- The big complaint by patients in the Denver area is that the closest MTFs that provide drugs are the Air Force Academy and Ft. Carson; both are in Colorado Springs. Buckley AF base has an MTF (albeit small), but it does not provide pharmacy coverage to the numerous dependents and retirees in the Denver area.

- It is not reasonable to refill prescriptions by mail/fax. When this is done, patients frequently do not return for office appointments and checkups on their blood pressure, glucose, etc.

- I suppose formularies are a necessary evil to contain costs. I find them, however, to be extremely burdensome. Most of my TRICARE patients have the mindset, "If I can't get it for free (or very cheap), I don't want it." I try to prescribe the best and safest medicine, which at times means it is more expensive. I would like to see doing away with blanket rejections and onerous obstacles. Instead, [I would like to see] a tiered system where the patients can still get what is best and safest for them just by paying a bit higher co-pay. Then, I would have to do fewer unnecessary lab tests and additional office visits, [and I would have] fewer hoops to jump through. Bureaucrats don't know why a certain medication is best for a certain patient. They don't know the long history of what has been tried and failed or associated with side effects already. I do.

TRICARE Program

- We are frustrated by TRICARE's abysmal reimbursement. Most doctors in this geographic area are not [TRICARE] providers because of this. We fought with TRICARE over depoprovera coverage. I have to buy 96 units of depo to get the lowest price of $41.20 each. TRICARE pays $45 plus $12 copay. What business can survive with such a narrow profit margin? TRICARE is the worst payer for depoprovera. [TRICARE] used to pay $31 [each], and I almost dropped my provider status over this. I feel military personnel should get the drugs prescribed at no cost to them. When I was in active duty, I served in the P&T committee and we were responsive to patient needs and costs; it worked well. But managed care P&T committees are dishonest, and I cannot deal with the myriad formularies shoved my way. I have never seen a TRICARE formulary.

- It is very difficult to find specialists to refer our TRICARE patients to. TRICARE takes a long time to approve our referrals. Of the hundreds of insurance companies we deal with in our office, TRICARE is by far the *worst* insurance company.

- I am a veteran. I have 3X years for pay purposes. I was a Navy corpsman during the Korean conflict, a Navy surgeon in Vietnam, and retired as an O-6 chief of surgery. I was recalled (from retired status) for Desert Shield/Desert Storm for most of 1991. Losing my private practice in the process, I was in civilian practice from 197X-197X, 198X-199X and since the end of 199X. I believe I'm in a position to judge, both from military and civilian standpoints, comparative medical systems. TRICARE is an abomination; virtually no physicians will accept TRICARE Prime due to the extremely low reimbursement rates. I haven't received an updated provider's directory in three years. The personnel at the local office are unresponsive and often rude. The referral process is by far the most cumbersome. To my knowledge, there is no intermediary "representative" between TRICARE and physicians. In brief, it is the worst third-party carrier with whom we deal.

- Most parents do not go to military facilities for drugs because the waiting time is *too long*, and when you have a sick child, you want to start treatment ASAP.

- I am very unhappy with the fact that the military base does not provide a copy of a formulary. I cannot prescribe medications on the formulary if I do not have knowledge of what is on the formulary! Furthermore, it is almost impossible to get any help by phoning them. They will not allow refills by phone or fax like real pharmacies. My patients are very upset when they drive 30-plus miles to the base to fill a prescription and are told that the prescription is not on their formulary. In my opinion it is a poor excuse for a pharmacy but I guess that the price is right!

- It is difficult to keep up with all the insurance companies' formularies. I always ask my patients if they know if a certain medication is available at [the MTF]. I do sign all of my prescriptions on the "product selection permitted" side [of the prescription form]; however, this seems unacceptable at the [MTF]. By signing this, it should allow the pharmacist to make the substitution. I don't have this problem with commercial pharmacies. We have more problems with TRICARE referrals than with the formulary.

- TRICARE provides poor coverage compared with other providers.

- I suppose formularies are a necessary evil to contain costs. I find them, however, to be extremely burdensome. Most of my TRICARE patients have the mind-set, "If I can't get it for free (or very cheap), I don't want it." I try to prescribe the best and safest medicine, which at times means it is more expensive. I would like to see doing away with blanket rejections and onerous obstacles. Instead, [I would like to see] a tiered system where the patients can still get what is best and safest for them just by paying a bit higher co-pay. Then, I would have to do fewer unnecessary lab tests and additional office visits, [and I would have] fewer hoops to jump through. Bureaucrats don't know why a certain medication is best for a certain patient. They don't know the long history of what has been tried and failed or associated with side effects already. I do.

- TRICARE management programs waste many hours of precious patient and staff time (e.g., attempting to micromanage first- and second-order clinical decision-making processes and testing). We are in the process of considering dropping this program because it [has a large] hassle factor and pre-approval, which wastes time, money, and efficiency. Actually [TRICARE's] drug program, which is full of micro-management holes, is better than their medical decision and pre-approval program—you should have run a survey for that!

Communication

- The formularies or preferred drug lists need to be in an easy-to-use format and on the Net or available through touch-tone phone—[then one could] spell out the medication to see if [it is] approved.

- Patients need to be *educated* as to (a) why they have a formulary and (b) what the cost of their *medications* is. They are currently too removed from the true cost of their health care, including drug costs.

- Provide the patient with a list of formulary alternatives for their problem.

- Justify formulary rejection to the provider and *patient*.

Miscellaneous

- I notice that my TRICARE patients are very well behaved and respectful compared with their peers—God Bless Our Military!

- Each health insurance product has a different formulary or preferred drug list and process for approving non-included medications. It is impossible for anyone to keep these lists current. If everything is equal, I will try to prescribe the covered or less-expensive drug, but often there are small but important differences [that would warrant prescribing] other medications. If the pharmacist or patient approached me regarding the alternative, I would be able to explain the reason for the choice. Systems that increase paperwork/staff time and patient activities decrease the use of needed medications, [but there] is still increased cost for health care [at a non-pharmacy level].

- I am retired from the Army, and even when I was on active duty I was unable to get a copy of the mail order formulary. I do keep copies of local military formularies when available but would love a copy of the mail order formulary and its prescribing rules. Thanks.

- The problem is taking the time to look up a patient's drug in all the different formularies we have to keep up with.

- The field of neurology—especially in epilepsy treatment—is changing rapidly. I do not feel that a formulary can keep up with rapidly evolving pharmacopeae.

- I am usually not aware of the type of insurance my patient has.

- Occasionally patients will say they're from the military base and are going to their pharmacy there. However, they have not mentioned any restrictions with formulary medicines.

- Military people and dependents deserve the best medical care for the job they do. They work in bad weather conditions, under lots of stress, and sometimes risk their lives for their country! Thanks.

- I have only had one military personnel patient, and he has moved out of town. I hate formularies. I have enough to do to practice medicine without the added burden of consulting formularies. I routinely throw away formularies!

- There are too many *different* formularies for different insurance companies.

References

Blumenthal, D., and R. Herdman, eds., *Description and Analysis of the VA National Formulary*, Institute of Medicine, Washington, D.C.: National Academy Press, 2000.

Bozzette S., R. D'Amato, S. Morton, K. Harris, R. Meili, and R. Taylor, *Pharmaceutical Technology Assessment for Managed Care: Current Practice Suggestions for Improvement*, Santa Monica, Calif.: RAND, MR-1206-SANOFI, 2001.

"Civilian Health and Medical Program of the Uniformed Services (CHAMPUS)/TRICARE; Implementation of the Pharmacy Benefits Program," *Federal Register*, Vol. 67, No. 71, April 12, 2002.

Dearing, C. J., T. A. Briscoe, S. M. Morgan, and L. C. Block, "Nifedipine-to-Felodipine Switch Program: Clinical and Economic Outcomes," *Formulary*, Vol. 33, No. 5, 1998, pp. 448–458.

"Department of Defense, Civilian Health and Medical Program of the Uniformed Services (CHAMPUS)/TRICARE, Implementation of the Pharmacy Benefits Program," *Federal Register*, Vol. 67, No. 71, April 12, 2002, pp. 17948–17954.

Donelan, K., et al., "The New Medical Marketplace: Physicians' Views," *Health Affairs*, Vol. 16, No. 5, 1997, pp. 139–148.

Flagstad, M. S., "Role of Pharmacy Benefit Management Companies in Integrated Health Care Systems," *Am J Health-Syst Pharm*, Vol. 53, Suppl., 1996, pp. S10–S13.

Foulke, G. E., and J. Siepler, "Antiulcer Therapy: An Exercise in Formulary Management," *J Clin Gastroenterol*, Vol. 12, Suppl., 1990, pp. S64–S68.

Futterman, R., H. Fillit, and J. L. Roglieri, "Use of Ineffective or Unsafe Medications Among Members of a Medicare HMO Compared to Individuals in a Medicare Fee-For-Service Program," *Am J Man Care*, Vol. 3, 1997, pp. 569–575.

Ganz, M. B., and B. Saksa, "Switching Long-Acting Nifedipine," *Fed Practitioner*, Vol. 14, No. 5, 1997, pp. 71, 72, 75.

Glassman, P. A., C. B. Good., M. E. Kelley., M. Bradley, M. Valentino, J. Ogden, and K. W. Kizer, "Physician Perceptions of a National Formulary," *Am J Manag Care*, Vol. 7, 2001, pp. 241–251.

Gold M., M. Joffe, T. L. Kennedy, and A. M. Tucker, "Pharmacy Benefits in Health Maintenance Organizations," *Health Affairs* Vol. 8, No. 3, 1989, pp. 182–190.

186

Hasty, M., J. Schrager, and K. Wrenn, "Physicians' Perceptions About Managed Care Restrictions on Antibiotic Prescribing," *J Gen Intern Med*, Vol. 14, 1999, pp. 756–758.

Hoescht, M. R., *Managed Care Digest Series 1999*, Kansas City, Mo.: Hoechst Marion Roussel, Vol. 3, 1999, pp. 40–41.

Hogan, C., P. B. Ginsburg, and J. R. Gabel, "Tracking Health Care Costs: Inflation Returns," *Health Tracking*, Vol. 19, No. 6, November/December 2000, pp. 217–223.

Horn, S. D., "The Clinical Practice Improvement (CPI) Model and How It Is Used to Examine the Availability of Pharmaceuticals and the Utilization of Ambulatory Healthcare Services in HMOs—Results from the Managed Care Outcomes Project (MCOP), *Pharmacoeconomics*, Vol. 10, Suppl. 2, 1996, pp. 50–55.

Horn, S. D., P. D. Sharkey, and C. Phillips-Harris, "Formulary Limitations and the Elderly: Results From the Managed Care Outcomes Project," *Am J Man Care*, Vol. 4, No. 8, 1998, pp. 1104–1113.

Horn, S. D., P. D. Sharkey, D. M. Tracy, C. E. Horn, B. James, and F. Goodwin, "Intended and Unintended Consequences of HMO Cost-Containment Strategies: Results From the Managed Care Outcomes Project," *Am J Man Care*, Vol. 2, 1996, pp. 253–264.

Kozma, C. M., C. E. Reeder, and E. W. Lingle, "Expanding Medicaid Drug Formulary Coverage: Effects on Utilization of Related Services," *Med Care*, Vol. 28, 1990, pp. 963–977.

Kravitz, R. L., and P. S. Romano, "Managed Care Cost Containment and the Law of Unintended Consequences," editorial, *Am J Man Care*, Vol. 2, 1996, pp. 323–324.

Kreling, D. H., and R. E. Mucha, "Drug Product Management in Health Maintenance Organizations," *Am J Hosp Pharm*, 1992, Vol. 49, 1992, pp. 374–381.

Lederle, F. A., and E. M. Rogers, "Lowering the Cost of Lowering Cholesterol: A Formulary Policy for Lovastatin," *J Gen Intern Med*, Vol. 5, 1990, pp. 459–463.

Long, S., *Regression Models for Categorical and Limited Dependent Variables*, Thousand Oaks, Calif.: Sage Publications, 1997.

Luce, B. R., and R. E. Brown, "The Use of Technology Assessment by Hospitals, Health Maintenance Organizations, and Third-Party Payers in the United States," *Int J Technol Assess Health Care*, Vol. 11, No. 1, Winter 1995, pp. 79–82.

Masia, N. A., "Pharmaceutical Innovation: Lowering the Price of Good Health," *Economic Realities in Health Care Policy*, Vol. 2, No. 2, 2002, pp. 3–13.

McCombs, J. S., and M. B. Nichol, "Pharmacy-Enforced Outpatient Drug Treatment Protocols: A Case Study of Medi-Cal Restrictions for Cefaclor," *Ann Pharmacother*, Vol. 27, 1993, pp. 155–161.

Mercer, William M., Inc., *Prescription Drug Coverage and Formulary Use in California: Different Approaches and Emerging Trends,* prepared for the California HealthCare Foundation, May 2001 (http://www.chcf.org/documents/providersystems/PrescriptionDrugCoverageandFormularyUse.pdf).

Mintzes, B., M. Barer, R. L. Kravitz, A. Kazanjian, K. Bassett, J. Lexchin, R. G. Evans, R. Pan., and S. A. Marion, "Influence of Direct to Consumer Pharmaceutical Advertising and Patients' Requests on Prescribing Decisions: Two Cite Cross Section Survey," *BMJ,* Vol. 324, 2002, pp. 278–279.

Monane, M., D. M. Mathithias, B. A. Nagle, and M. A. Kelly, "Improving Prescribing Patterns for the Elderly Through an Online Drug Utilization Review Intervention: A System Linking the Physician, Pharmacist, and Computer," *JAMA,* Vol. 280, 1998, pp. 1249–1252.

Motheral, B. R., and R. Henderson, "The Effect of a Closed Formulary on Prescription Drug Use and Costs," *Inquiry,* Vol. 36, 2000, pp. 481–491.

Newhouse, J. P., and the RAND Health Insurance Experiment Group, *Free for All,* Cambridge, Mass.: Harvard University Press, 1994.

Patel, R. J., D. R. Gray, R. Pierce, and M. Jafari, "Impact of Therapeutic Interchange from Pravastatin to Lovastatin in a Veterans Affairs Medical Center," *Am J Managed Care,* Vol. 5, 1999, pp. 465–474.

Rahal, J. J., et al., "Class Restriction of Cephalosporin Use to Control Total Cephalosporin Resistance in Nosocomial Klebsiella," *JAMA,* Vol. 280, 1998, pp. 1233–1237.

Rosenthal, M. B., E. R. Berndt, J. M. Donohue, R. G. Frank, and A. M. Epstein, "Promotion of Prescription Drugs to Consumers," *NEJM,* Vol. 346, 2002, pp. 498–505.

Ross-Degnan, D., and S. B. Soumerai, "HMO Formularies and Care Costs," letter, *Lancet,* Vol. 347, 1996, p. 1264.

Rucker, T. D., and G. Schiff, "Drug Formularies: Myths-in-Formation," *Med Care,* Vol. 28, 1990, pp. 928–942.

Schectman, J. M., E. Q. Elinsky, N. K. Kanwal, and J. E. Ott, "HMO Physician Attitudes Toward Drug Cost Containment Strategies," *HMO Practice,* Vol. 9, No. 3, 1995, pp. 116–119.

Schulman, K. A., L. E. Rubinstein, D. R. Abernethy, D. M. Seils, and D. P. Sulmasy, "The Effect of Pharmaceutical Benefits Managers: Is It Being Evaluated," *Ann Intern Med,* Vol. 124, 1996, pp. 906–913.

Smalley, W. E., M. R. Griffin, R. L. Fought, L. Sullivan, and W. A. Ray, "Effect of a Prior-Authorization Requirement on the Use of Nonsteroidal Anti-inflammatory Drugs by Medicaid Patients," *N Engl J Med,* Vol. 332, 1995, pp. 1612–1617.

Soumerai, S. B., D. Ross-Degnan, J. Avorn, T. J. McLaughlin, and I. Choodnovskiy, "Effects of Medicaid Drug-Payment Limits on Admission to Hospitals and Nursing Homes," *New Engl J Med*, Vol. 325, 1991, pp. 1072–1077.

Strunk, B. C., P. B. Ginsburg, and J. R. Gabel, "Tracking Health Care Costs: Hospital Care Key Cost Driver in 2000," Center for Studying Health Care System Change, *Data Bulletin 21*, September (2001, http://www.hschange. org/CONTENT/372/).

Teitlebaum, F., A. Parker, R. Martinez, and C. Rowe, *Drug Trend Report*, Express Scripts, Inc., June 1999.

U.S. Department of Health and Human Services, *Report to the President: Prescription Coverage, Spending, Utilization, and Prices*, Washington, D.C.: DHHS, April 2000.

U.S. General Accounting Office, *Defense Health Care: Fully Integrated Pharmacy System Would Improve Service and Cost-Effectiveness*, HEHS-98-176, June 12, 1998.

U.S. General Accounting Office, *Defense Health Care: Need for Top-to-Bottom Redesign of Pharmacy Programs*, T-HEHS-99-75, March 10, 1999a.

U.S. General Accounting Office, *Defense Health Care: Pharmacy Copayments*, HEHS-99-134R, June 8, 1999b.

U.S. General Accounting Office, *VA Drug Formulary: Better Oversight Is Required, but Veterans Are Getting Needed Drugs*, Washington, D.C., GAO-01-183, January 2001 (available from GAO at www.gao.gov).

Walser, B. L., D. Ross-Degnan, and S. B. Soumerai, "Do Open Formularies Increase Access to Clinically Useful Drugs?" *Health Affairs*, Vol. 15, No. 3, 1996, pp. 95–109.

Weiner, J. P., A. Lyles, and D. M. Steinwachs, "Impact of Managed Care on Prescription Drug Use," *Health Affairs*, Vol. 10, No. 1, 1991, pp. 140–154.

William M. Mercer, Inc., *Prescription Drug Coverage and Formulary Use in California: Different Approaches and Emerging Trends*, prepared for the California Healthcare Foundation (www.chcf.org), May 2001.